AWS CERTIFIED SOLUTIONS ARCHITECT ASSOCIATE STUDY GUIDE:

The Ultimate Cheat Sheet Practice Exam Questions with Answers & Detailed Explanations For The Latest SAA-C01 Exam

Barry Adams

© Copyright 2020 - All rights reserved.

TABLE OF CONTENTS

Introduction:

Were you prepared to find out additional? Associate with the AWS engineer network, advance your insight into the web and in-person training, exhibit your ability with confirmations, and investigate reference materials to expand on AWS.

Interface with Engineer Networks

The worldwide AWS environment comprises a scope of AWS fans and backers, who are enthusiastic about helping other people construct.

Client Gatherings

Join an AWS people group close to you to learn, system, and offer distributed computing enthusiasm.

AWS Heroes

Find out about the lively overall network of master clients and influencers.

Virtual People Group

Add your voice to the AWS dialogs occurring in different online networks.

AWS Events

Interface, work together, and gain from specialists on the web and in-person AWS occasions.

Develop Your Range of Abilities

Whether you are only interested in AWS or a prepared star, you have a vast information base.

AWS Online Tech Talks

Stream online introductions and workshops drove by AWS arrangements modelers and specialists.

AWS Partner Network TV

Watch sessions, meetings, demos, and all the more, including AWS and APN Partners.

Get Prepared and Confirmed

Gain from AWS specialists. Advance your aptitudes and information. Manufacture your future in the AWS Cloud.

Computerized and Study Hall Preparing

Learn with free computerized preparing or increase hands-on involvement with a live homeroom.

Accreditation Tests

Acquire qualifications and exhibit your AWS aptitude to bosses and companions.

Investigate Reference Materials

Handy reference materials can help you expand AWS. Before we start, first, let me introduce you to the AWS SAA-C02 exam domain. The examination base on these four domains. Part one is to design Resilient Architectures. Part 2 is to create High-performance Architecture. In domain 3, we will look at how Secure Applications and Architectures can build. Domain 4 is the development of Cost-Optimized Architectures.

Therefore, each of these domains splits into several percentages, i.e., the questions will make up this percentage. For example, Domain one will have 30 percent of the examination. Domain two will cover 28 percent, domain three will have 24 percent, and domain four will have 18 percent of the study. You can see the parts and respective objectives in the following images. It is all about four domains. Let's get started with our prep book.

Domain 1: Design Resilient Architectures 30%

Domain 2: Design High-Performing Architectures 28%

Domain 3: Design Secure Applications and Architectures 24%

Domain 4: Design Cost-Optimized Architectures 18%

TOTAL 100%

Domain 1: Resilient Design Architectures

1.1 Design a multi-tier architecture solution

1.2 Design highly available and fault-tolerant architectures

1.3 Design decoupling mechanisms using AWS services

1.4 Choose appropriate resilient storage

Domain 2: Design High-Performing Architectures

2.1 Identify elastic and scalable compute solutions for a workload

2.2 Select high-performing and scalable storage solutions for a workload

2.3 Select high-performing networking solutions for a workload

2.4 Choose high-performing database solutions for a workload

Domain 3: Design Secure Applications and Architectures

3.1 Design secure access to AWS resources

3.2 Design secure application tiers

3.3 Select appropriate data security options

Domain 4: Design Cost-Optimized Architectures

4.1 Identify cost-effective storage solutions

4.2 Identify cost-effective compute and database services

4.3 Design cost-optimized network architectures

- AWS course and exam resources

- Benefits of becoming on AWS certified solutions architect

CHAPTER 1:

Compute

Instance Pricing

Instance, pricing is significant to know when you're looking at cost-optimized compute options in AWS.

On-demand instances: This is good when you have development and test environments and when you want cases for a brief period.

Let's say you have a test environment for a month or a developer environment for say two months; then you should use on-demand

Spot instances: Use this when you have batch processing activities - activities that can survive interruption. We place a high price on the spot instance, and if you lose the bit, you lose the sample. There are other capabilities such as hibernation, but when it comes to the exams, understand that it's only useful when you have batch processing activities to use a spot instance.

Reserved instances: When you know that you need servers 24/7 throughout the year, you can save costs by purchasing reserved capacity.

Dedicated instances: Here, the example runs on hardware that dedicates to a particular customer. It could be a company with multiple AWS accounts, and they have hardware that saves them. If the customer has multiple AWS accounts, then launched across these accounts will share the same hardware.

Dedicated hosts: You have complete control over the physical server. It uses cases where you have a third party application wherein the licensing bases on the number of cores. I have seen applications with a strict policy on licensing that you need to have a physical course as part of the contract; in such a case, you have to use a dedicated host. Or maybe you have a security policy which mandates that you cannot share infrastructure with any other instances; in such a case, you have to use a dedicated host.

Serverless Compute

AWS Lambda

- This is good when you don't want to manage the underlying infrastructure.

- In AWS Lambda, you only get billed for how much of use

- It's effortless to port your existing code and save on the cost by using AWS lambda because you don't need to worry about the costing of your underlying EBS volume or your underlying issue instance.

- Normally, this lambda function is used along with the API gateway; so if you get a question on the combination of services, it's always the API gateway and the AWS lambda.

- You can create APIs in the API gateway service, which can be invoked by customers. Then you can have the APS invoke the lambda functions internally.

Elastic Container Service

It is under operational excellence because we now have microservices, and many organizations are using microservices to design their architecture.

- Elastic container service uses for orchestration of your containers. Instead of installing an orchestration service like Kubernetes on EC2, you can use the elastic container service to manage all the docker containers.

Here you define something known as types; for the kind, you mention the image that needs to pulls down - this could be pulled out from the docker hub or from the elastic container s3, which is available in AWS. It deploys containers on managed instances then you can access all of this via service.

It is all done automatically for you in the elastic container service, as it's a fully managed service. It also has auto-scaling capabilities. If you want orchestration to be handled entirely for you with auto-scaling capabilities, you have to use the Elastic Container Service.

REVIEW QUESTIONS

Question 1:

When the object uploads to the Amazon S3 bucket, you want to run some code. How do I do this?

1. Create an event notification on the S3 bucket that triggered the Lambda function

2. Configure Lambda to poll the S3 bucket for changes and run a role when it finds new objects

3. Create an event notification on the S3 bucket to notify Amazon SNS to trigger the Lambda function

Question 2:

Which type of Amazon storage service uses a standards-based REST web interface to manage objects?

1. Amazon Elastic File System (EFS)

2. Amazon Elastic Block Store (EBS)

3. Amazon Simple Storage Service (S3)

4. Amazon FSx for Windows File Server

Question 3:

Which EC2 pricing model would you use for a short-term requirement that needs to complete over a weekend?

1. Reserved Instance

2. Spot Instance

3. Dedicated Instance

4. On-Demand Instance

Question 4:

How do you create a hierarchy that mimics the file system in Amazon S3?

1. Create buckets within other buckets

2. Use folders in your buckets

3. Upload objects within other objects

4. Use lifecycle rules to tier your data

Question 5:

A new application requires a database that can write to DB instances in multiple availability zones with reading after write consistency. Which solution meets these requirements?

1. Amazon Aurora Global Database

2. Amazon Aurora Replicas

3. Amazon Aurora Cross-RegionReplicas

4. Amazon Aurora Multi-Master

Question 6:

A customer needs a schema-less database that can seamlessly scale. Which AWS database service would you recommend?

1. Amazon DynamoDB

2. Amazon ElastiCache

3. Amazon RDS

4. Amazon Aurora

Question 7:

Which DynamoDB feature integrates with AWS Lambda to automatically execute functions in response to table updates?

1. DynamoDB Global Tables

2. DynamoDB Auto Scaling

3. DynamoDB Streams

4. DynamoDB DAX

Question 8:

Which of the following is a fair use case for Amazon RedShift?

1. Schema-less transactional database

2. Relational data warehouse

3. Relational transactional database

4. Analytics using the Hadoop framework

Question 9:

Which Amazon ElastiCache engine provides data persistence?

1. Redis

2. Memcached

Question 10:

At what level do you attach the Internet gateway?

1. Public Subnet

2. Private Subnet

3. Availability Zone

4. VPC

Question 11:

What is the scope of the virtual private cloud (VPC)?

1. Global

2. Regional

3. Availability Zone

Question 12:

The architect needs to point the domain name dctlabs.com to the DNS name of Elastic Load Balancer. Which record type should use?

1. MX record

2. A record

3. CNAME record

4. Alias record

Question 13:

Which of the following listener/protocol combination is incorrect?

1. Application Load Balancer TCP and HTTP/HTTPS

2. Classic Load Balancer TCP and HTTP/HTTPS

3. Network Load Balancer TCP

Question 14:

What type of scaling does Amazon EC2 Auto Scaling provide?

1. Vertical

2. Horizontal

Question 15:

An organization needs a private, high-bandwidth, low-latency connection to the AWS Cloud to establish a hybrid cloud configuration with its on-premises cloud. What type of relationship should they use?

1. AWS Managed VPN

2. AWS VPN CloudHub

3. AWS Direct Connect

4. Transit VPC

Question 16:

An architect is designing a web application that has locations in multiple regions around the world. The architect wants to provide automatic routing to the nearest area and can failover to other areas. The customer should obtain 2 IP addresses for the whitelist. How do I do this?

1.   Use Route 53 latency-based routing

2.   Use Amazon CloudFront

3.   Use AWS Global Accelerator

4.   Use Route 53 geolocation routing

Question 17:

What services does Amazon API Gateway use for its public terminals?

1.   AWS Lambda

2.   Amazon CloudFront

3.   Amazon S3

4.   Amazon ECS

Question 18:

A company provides videos for new employees around the world. They need to store the videos in one location and then offer low-latency access for the employees around the world. Which service would be best suited to providing fast access to the content?

1. Amazon S3

2. AWS Global Accelerator

3. Amazon CloudFront

4. AWS Lambda

CHAPTER 2:

Storage

Amazon S3 (Simple Storage Service)

These are everything that you will need to manage your data in specific clusters. AWS refers to these clusters of data that you are accessing, caring, and moving as buckets. You will effectively designate several pieces of information or data as one particular bucket. You can then move that bucket around.

These four storage systems are Amazon Standard Storage, Amazon Infrequent Access Storage, Amazon Glacier, and Amazon Reduced Redundancy Storage.

Amazon Standard Storage

It is perfect for data that you need quick access to and is readily available. For example, you may want specific media files used regularly to stores within Amazon Standard Storage, thanks to how readily available and cheap storage is. This data can manage within Amazon Standard Storage. It means that your bill will be based entirely on how much information you use rather than having to buy a specific amount and worrying about data caps.

Amazon Infrequent Access Storage

Resources that you still require for functioning that are less frequently accessed can stores in Amazon Infrequent Access Storage. Data stored here is always readily available but is stored far cheaper. Unlike Amazon Standard Storage, which has an availability of 99.99% of the time (which calculates to less than an hour of downtime within a year), Amazon Infrequent Access Storage is readily available 99.9% of the time, making it down for less than 9 hours a year. If those extra 8 hours of downtime a year are not a concern for you, using Amazon Infrequent Access Storage instead can be a way to save some money.

Amazon Glacier

This third form of data storage allows for the storage of information that is rarely accessed but must be stored. For example, you may use this to keep the work records you rarely need or store backups. It should be information that you will not need instantly. Instead, it should only be for archives of data that you must maintain because it can take significantly longer to retrieve. Think of this data as being stored in a deep freezer—you cannot just instantly thaw it out because you decide you want it right then. Instead, it would help if you waited, and with Amazon Glacier, you sometimes have to wait hours for your archives to thaw out. However, another benefit is that the data stored in Glacier becomes redundant, which means that it is stored in multiple different sites worldwide, allowing you to rest with peace of mind, even in the event of natural disasters or failures in any particular location. You can also use it with confidence.

Amazon Reduced Redundancy Storage

Amazon Reduced Redundancy Storage is meant to store easily reproducible data and is not considered essential to functioning. It is data that is readily available without any real redundancy. It means that it is more vulnerable to loss than the other forms, but it also allows for cheaper storage.

Elastic Block Store

AWS Elastic Block Store (EBS) allows for the storage volumes to provide low latency. The range of workloads provides for several different processes to be included and possible with EBS, such as:

• Relational and non-relational databases

• Containerized applications

• File systems

• Enterprise applications

• Data analytics engines

When utilizing EBS, you give the option between four different types that will allow you to choose an option that balances your price range with the performance you wish to achieve. You will see functions and systems that can process data nearly instantly with single digit-millisecond latency. EBS can find in four forms: General Purpose SSD, Provisioned IOPS SSD, Throughput Optimized HDD, and Cold HDD.

Snowball

The recommended solution for moving the most amounts of on-premises data to the AWS cloud as fast as possible is AWS Snowball. It is an appliance-based storage device shipped to the tenant where up to 50 TB data can be loaded. The appliance sends back to the tenant where AWS receives it and copies data over AWS S3 storage. There is support for multiple devices with concurrent data transfers and 256-bit encryption of data at rest. Snowball recommendsreplacing AWS Import/Export, particularly with data transfers larger than 10 TB to S3 buckets. Snowball jobs create from the AWS management console, and a Snowball appliance is automatically shipped on-premises.

Elastic File System (EFS)

Elastic File System enables what is essentially a file server in the Cloud. The EFS is associated with a single VPC where users with security permissions can access and share files. The Elastic File System is a managed service created and mounted on single or multiple Linux-based EC2 instances to enable data file storage and sharing. EFS provides file locking and strong consistency that is characteristic of a file system. There is also support for mounting EFS file systems within your VPC to any on-premises servers for migrating, backup, or workload purposes. It allows thousands of EC2 instances to upload, access, delete, and share files simultaneously.

AWS Storage Gateway

Amazon AWS Storage Gateway is a hybrid solution that supports storing some or all of the data locally to improve performance. AWS Storage Gateway is a software (virtual) device deployed locally that provides native encryption of tenant data. The following is a list of AWS storage gateway options that store some or all cloud data.

• Stored Volume Gateway

• Cached Volume Gateway

• Tape Gateway (VTL)

REVIEW QUESTIONS

Question 1

For non-relational databases,which is the best AWS Service?

Choose one out of four.

A.   Amazon Glacier

B.   Amazon DynamoDB

C.   Amazon Redshift

D.   Amazon RDS

Question 2

Amazon ElastiCache supports which of the following cache engines?

Choose two out of four.

A.   Memcached

B.   Couchbase

C.   MySQL

D.   Redis

Question 3

From the actions below, which IAM policies can control ones?

Choose three out of five.

A.   Creating an Amazon S3 bucket

B.   Logging into .NET applications

C.   Creating tables in a MySQL RDS database

D.   Configuring a VPC security group

E.   Creating an Oracle RDS database

Question 4

A t2.medium EC2 instance type launches with what kind of Amazon Machine Image (AMI)?

A. An Instance store Hardware Virtual Machine AMI

B. An Instance store Paravirtual AMI

C. An Amazon EBS-backed Hardware Virtual Machine AMI

D. An Amazon EBS-backed Paravirtual AMI

Question 5

To launch a fully configured instantly, what is the template that Auto Scaling would use?

Choose one out of four.

A.   User data

B.   Launch configuration

C.   Keypair

D.   Instance type

Question 6

Of the options below, which are characteristics of the AWS Auto Scaling Service?

Choose two out of six.

A.   Collects and tracks metrics and sets alarms

B.   Delivers push notifications

C.   Sends traffic to healthy instances

D.   Enforces a minimum number of running Amazon EC2 instances

E.   Responds to changing conditions by adding or terminating Amazon EC2 instances.

F.   Launches instances from a specified Amazon Machine Image (AMI).

Question 7

A customer needs a file, such as a PDF file made available to be publicly downloadable. The PDF file is going to be downloaded by customers using their browsers. The PDF file will be downloaded in this manner millions of times. From the options below, which will be the most cost-effective for the customer?

Choose one out of four.

A.   Store the file in Glacier

B.   Store the file in EFS

C.   Store the file in S3 Standard

D.   Store the file in S3 Standard-IA

Question 8

A mobile phone application runs statistical articles from individual files in an Amazon S3 bucket. There are articles older than 40 days that no more extended needs for the application and items over 30 days old that are hardly ever read. These articles are no longer required to be visible through the mobile application. Still, the archive for historical data purposes.

From the list below, select the cost-effective solution that best meets these requirements.

Choose one out of four.

A.   For files older than 30 days, create lifecycle rules to move these files to Amazon S3 Standard Infrequent Access and use Amazon Glacier to move files older than 40 days.

B.   For files more aged than 30 days, create a Lambda function to force them to Amazon Glacier and move files older than 40 days to Amazon EBS.

C.   Create a Lambda function that moves files to Amazon EBS that are older than 30 days and transfer files to Amazon Glacier older than 40 days.

D.   For files more aged than 30 days, create lifecycle rules to move these files to Amazon Glacier and use Amazon S3 Standard Infrequent Access to move files older than 40 days to.

Question 9

A Solutions Architect is designing a log-processing solution that requires storage that supports up to 500 MB/s throughput. An Amazon EC2 instance sequentially accesses the data.

Which Amazon storage type satisfies these requirements?

Choose one out of four.

A.   EBS Cold HDD (sc1)

B.   EBS Provisioned IOPS SSD (io1)

C.   EBS General Purpose SSD (gp2)

D.   EBS Throughput Optimized HDD (st1)

CHAPTER 3:

Networking

VPC sizing and structure

VPC consideration

• How big should the VPC be. It will limit usage.

• Are there networks that cannot use?

• Pay attention to the ranges used by other VPCs or used in different cloud environments.

• Try to predict future uses.

• VPC structure with levels and zones of resilience (availability)

• VPC min /28 network (16 IP)

• VPC max /16 (65456 IP)

How to size VPC

A subnet is in an availability zone. Try to divide each subnet into levels (application, web, database, reservation). Since each region has at least three AZs, it is good to separate the network into four different AZs.

It allows at least one subnet in each AZ and one reservation. Taking a /16 subnet and dividing it into 16 shapes will make each one a /20.

VPC subnets

AZ Strong VPC subnet.

• If the Available zone fails, the subnet and services also fail.

• High availability requires multiple components in different AZs.

• One subnet can only have 1 AZ.

• 1 AZ can have zero or more subnets.

• CIDR IPv4 is a subset of the VID CIDR block.

• Impossible to overlap with other subnets in that VPC

• Optionally, the IPv6 CIDR block can assign to the subnet.

• (256/64 subnets can adapt to /56 VPC)

• Subnets can interact with other subnets in the VPC by default.

VPC Routing and Internet Gateway

VPC Router is a high availability device available in every VPC that moves traffic from one place to another. The router has a network interface on each subnet of the VPC. Route traffic between subnets. Routing tables define what the VPC router will do with the traffic when the data leaves that subnet. A VPC creates a primary route table. If a custom route table is not associated with a subnet, it uses the main route table of the VPC.

NAT - Network Address Translation Gateway

Set of diverse processes that can address IP packets by alternating their source or destination addresses. It allows many IPv4 lessons to use a public IP for outgoing access to the Internet. Incoming connections don't work. Outgoing links can get a returned response.

• It must be run from a public subnet to allow the public IP address.

o Internet Gateway subnets configure to assign available IPv4 addresses and default routes for those subnets that point to IGW.

• Use elastic IP (public static IPv4)

o Do not change

o Assigned to your account

• Resilient service AZ, but HA in that AZ.

o If that Available zon=e fails, there is no recovery.

REVIEW QUESTIONS

Question 1:

On Friday morning, your marketing manager calls an urgent meeting to celebrate that they have secured a deal to run a coordinated national promotion on TV, radio, and social media over the next ten days.

They anticipate a 500x increase in site visits and trial registrations. After the meeting, you throw some ideas around with your team about ensuring that your current one server web site will survive.

Which of these best embodies the AWS design strategy for this situation? [Select 2]

A) Work with your web design team to create web pages with embedded java scripts to emulate your five most popular information web pages and sign up web pages.

B) Upgrade your existing server from a 1xlarge to a 32xlarge for the duration of the campaign.

C) Create a stand by sign up a server to use if the primary fails due to load.

D) Create a duplicate sign up page that stores registration details in DynamoDB for asynchronous processing using SQS & Lambda.

E) Work with your web design team to create web pages in PHP to run on a 32xlarge EC2 instance to emulate your five most popular information web pages and sign up web pages.

F) Recreate your five most popular new customer web pages and sign up web pages on LightSail and take advantage of AWS auto-scaling to pick up the load.

Question 2:

A software development company has recently invested 20 million dollars in building their artificial intelligence APIs and AI-powered chatbots.

You are hired as a Solutions Architect to build a low-cost prototype on their AWS cloud infrastructure. Which of the following AWS service combinations will provide user authentication, scalable object storage, and allow you to run code without having to host it in an EC2 instance?

A) Cognito, Lambda, S3

B) AWS IoT, Cognito, S3

C) IAM, Lambda, EBS Volumes

D) IAM, Cognito, EBS Volumes

Question 3:

When using EC2 instances with Dedicated Hosting, which of the following modes are you able to transition between by stopping the model and starting it again?

A) Dedicated & Default

B) Non-Dedicated & Dedicated

C) Host & Default

D) Dedicated & Host

Question 4:

Which of the following are valid Route 53 routing policies? [Select 3]

A) Latency

B) Multitarget answer

C) Simple

D) Weighted

E) Complex

F) Shortest First

Question 5:

You have an EC2 instance that is transferring data from S3 in the same region.

The project sponsor is worried about the cost of the infrastructure. What can you do to convince him that you have a cost-effective solution?

A) You are going to be hosting only four instances, so you are minimizing cost.

B) There is no cost for transferring data from EC2 to S3 if they are in the same region.

C) AWS provides a discount if you transfer data from EC2 to S3 if they are in the same region.

D) Both EC2 and S3 are in the same availability zone so that you can save via consolidated billing.

Question 6:

What are the data formats used to create CloudFormation templates? [Select 2]

A) XML

B) YAML

C) CSV

D) JSON

Question 7:

A company has a solution hosted in AWS. This solution consists of a set of EC2 instances. They have been recently getting attacks as their IT security departments identified that attacks are from a group of IP addresses. Which of the following methods can be adopted to help in this situation?

A) Place the EC2 instances into private subnets and set up a NAT gateway so employees can access them.

B) Remove the IGW from the VPC so that no outside traffic can reach the EC2 instances.

C) Lockdown of NACL for the set to IP address.

D) Place the EC2 instances into private subnets and set up a bastion host so employees can access them.

Question 8:

Which of the following Amazon S3 Storage Classes offer 99.999999999% (11 x 9s) durability?

A) Standards are not frequently accessed, and an area is not frequently accessed, reducing redundant storage

B) Standard, Standard-Infrequent Access, One Zone-Infrequent Access

C) Reduced Redundancy Storage, Standard, One Zone-Infrequent Access

D) Standard, Glacier, Reduced Redundancy Storage

Question 9:

You work for a genomics company developing a cure for motor neuron disease by using advanced gene therapies. As a part of their research, they take massive data sets (usually in the terabytes) and analyze these data sets using Elastic Map Reduce. To keep costs low, they run the analysis for only a few hours in the early hours of the morning, using spot instances for the task nodes. The core nodes are on-demand instances. Lately, however, the EMR jobs have been failing. It is due to spot instances unexpectedly terminate. Which of the following remedies would keep costs manageable and mitigate the issues caused by terminated spot instances? [Select 2]

A) Change the core nodes to spot cases and lower the spot price.

B) Increase the bid price for the core nodes.

C) Change the task nodes to on-demand instances.

D) Increase the bid price for the task nodes to have a more significant threshold before the task nodes terminate.

Question 10:

Amazon Web Services offers four different levels of support. Which of the following are reasonable support levels? [Select 3]

A) Business

B) Enterprise

C) Developer

D) Corporate

E) Free Tier

Question 11:

Which of the following AWS services encrypts data at rest by default? (Choose 2)

A) AWS Storage Gateway

B) Amazon RDS

C) Amazon DynamoDB

D) Amazon Glacier

Question 12:

You work for a large software company in Seattle.

They configured a production environment on AWS on a custom VPC. VPC includes public subnets and private subnets.

The company tests its applications on custom EC2 instances in a private subnet. There are approximately 500 instances, and they communicate to the outside world via a proxy server. At 3am every night, the EC2 instances pull-down OS updates, usually 150MB or so. They then apply these updates and reboot: if the software has not downloaded within half an hour, the update will attempt to download the following day. Which of the following answers might explain this failure? [Select 2]

A) Your proxy server is blacklisting the address from which the updates download, resulting in failed downloads.

B) The proxy server is located in a private subnet and uses a NAT instance to connect to the Internet. However, this instance is too small to handle the required network traffic. You should re-provision the NAT solution so that it's able to handle the throughput.

C) The proxy server has only one elastic IP address added to it. To increase network throughput, you should add additional elastic IP addresses.

D) The proxy server has an inadequately sized EBS volume attached to it. The network buffer stores on the EBS volume, and it is running out of disk space when trying to ease the 500 simultaneous connections. You should provision an EBS volume with provisioned IOPS.

E) The proxy server is on an inadequately sized EC2 instance.

It does not have sufficient network throughput to handle all updates simultaneously. You should increase the instance size or type of the EC2 model for the proxy server.

Question 13:

Which of the following AWS services allow native encryption of data while at rest? [Select 3]

A) ElastiCache for Memcached

B) Elastic Block Store (EBS)

C) S3

D) Elastic File System (EFS)

Question 14:

You are consulting with a mid-sized company with a predominantly Mac & Linux desktop environment.

In passing, they comment that they have over 30TB of unstructured Word and spreadsheet documents, of which 85% of these documents don't get accessed again after about 35 days. They wish they could find a quick and easy solution to have tiered storage to store these documents more cost-effectively without impacting staff access.

What options can you offer them? [Select 2]

A) Migrate documents to File Gateway presented as iSCSI and made use of life-cycle using Infrequent Access storage.

B) Migrate the document store to S3 storage and make use of life-cycle using Infrequent Access storage.

C) Migrate documents to EFS storage and make use of life-cycle using Infrequent Access storage.

D) Migrate documents to File Gateway presented as NFS and made use of life-cycle using Infrequent Access storage.

Question 15:

A single m4. Medium NAT instance inside a VPC supports a company of 100 people. This NAT instance allows individual EC2 models in private subnets to communicate out to the internet without being directly accessible via the internet. As the company has grown over the past year, they have discovered that the additional traffic passing through the NAT instance is causing severe performance degradation. What might you do to solve this problem?

A) Instead of using a NAT, use Direct Connect to route all traffic through your VPC and back out to the Internet.

B) Attach an additional IGW to your VPC.

C) Increase the class size of the NAT instance from an m4.medium to an m4.xLarge.

D) Use an Elastic Load Balancer and forward traffic out through this ELB. The ELB will automatically scale on-demand as traffic increases.

CHAPTER 4:

Content delivery

Amazon Route 53

Amazon Route 53 is the built-in AWS DNS service. It is responsible for the time and price-efficient routing of DNS (domain name system). The internet can convert the URL into a web browser into an IP address associated with that URL. Effectively, this is the program that will allow for access to the webpages.

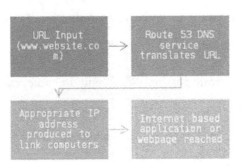

Route 53 design work in tandem with other AWS infrastructure—in particular, it is efficient when utilized with;

Amazon EC2 instances

• ELB load balancers

- Amazon S3 buckets

- Outside infrastructure

Thanks to its flexibility, you can use Route 53 to make sure that traffic makes it to the proper endpoint, as well as to monitor whether requests redirect appropriately, arriving at their endpoint without issue. There are several other functions to keep track of and manage traffic on your domain, such as:

- Latency based routing: Route 53 balances out the traffic load so that latency does not overwhelm one or two endpoints.

- GeoDNS: You can route customers to specific domains based on the customer's location based on the location services within the device used.

- Geoproximity: Users will be routed based on the physical distance between the user and the resources, causing users to access the closest data center.

- Weighted round-robin: You will be able to specify specific weights or traffic loads that can be handled by each server, route more traffic that can operate without overwhelming servers that not be able to withstand the same traffic.

The above information is stored in the program Amazon Route 53 Traffic Flow, which allows you to perform all monitoring in one place. It can also be used in conjunction with DNS failover to achieve a low-latency and fault-tolerant architecture to keep servers and domains running.As one last point, Amazon Route 53 also provides for domain name registration. You can directly purchase your domain names through AWS, and Route 53 will take care of configuring the DNS settings for you.

CloudFront

Amazon CloudFront allows the delivery of content globally. It utilizes the massive global infrastructure that Amazon has built up to provide high speed and low cost. It will enable the content to keep closer to the user than ever, allowing for a better experience using the products, thanks to receiving content quicker than ever. Virtually, its design to be low-latency with a high transfer rate while also being incredibly developer-friendly. It is built into AWS and works smoothly and effectively with all other AWS products and services. Even better, if you are already using AWS origins for the data, such as having it processed from Amazon S3, EC2, or ELB, you will not have to pay for the transfer of data from those services CloudFront instance you are using.

This service comes with several key benefits that make it fantastic to utilize your AWS services:

• Global without sacrificing speed: It utilizes global distribution on a massive scale, with 200 points of presence while relying on Amazon's network for wide availability for the users of your programs or websites.

• Secure: Despite several security concerns, CloudFront is mostly secure, with both in-network protection and protection on the application level. It includes Amazon Shield Standard with the program itself and configurable settings, such as AWS Certificate Manager and custom SSL certificates, without spending extra.

• Customizable: It is mainly programmable and customizable to fit what your application requires. Your code can be spread across several AWS locations worldwide to increase response times and integrate it with several other tools.

• Already integrated within AWS: Thanks to being a part of the AWS arsenal, it connects with other AWS services. Your CloudFront operations can be accessed in the same console as your other AWS services, making it a popular choice.

CloudWatch

The last of the AWS Essential services is CloudWatch. It is effectively your monitoring hub. When you use CloudWatch, you can monitor the AWS applications that you are utilizing. It allows you to see statistics and usage in near-real-time for your essential services, such as:

• Amazon Elastic Compute Cloud instances

• Amazon Elastic Block Store volumes

• Amazon Relational Database Service

• Elastic Load Balancers

It works because it can collect data, monitor your applications and infrastructure, act accordingly, and analyze your AWS infrastructure, services, and applications.

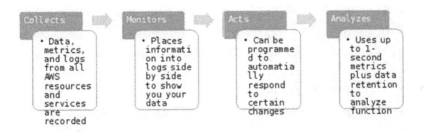

Thanks to the fact that it automatically integrates with AWS, you are set up to use it quickly and simply, allowing you to read statistics and metrics on latency, the current usage of CPU, request counts, and more. You will be able to track the health of your application, the number of resources used, any issues that may arise, and any restrictions encountered.

Because you have all of this information readily available, you can solve any IT issues that come up with ease.

CloudWatch is mainly integrated into EC2, providing two different levels of monitoring based on what works best for you. These are:

• Basic Monitoring: No added fees—this also includes seven metrics of your choice that runs every 5 minutes, and three status-check metrics run every 1 minute.

• Detailed Monitoring: Has added fees—this allows you to make sure that all metrics increase to occurring in 1-minute intervals.

Beyond just that, CloudWatch monitors the following:

- Latency within EBS

- Storage space and freeable memory metrics within the RDS database

- Messages sent and received within SQS queues

- The number of delivered messages through SNS topics

CloudWatch can also be customized to provide the client with a graph of data within AWS services—both real-time and data logged over the last two weeks. It is also possible to create alarms and notifications whenever any metrics are outside of specified ranges and when resources did not utilize to their potential. It can even involve customizing some specific responses to certain parameters that can automatize.

REVIEW QUESTIONS

Question 1

Which of the following options enables users to access private files in S3 in a secure manner? (Choose three)

a)   CloudFront-origin access identity

b)   CloudFront-signed URLs

c)   Public S3 buckets

d)   CloudFront-signed cookies

Question 2

Which is not part of a Cloud Adoption Framework component?

a)   Creation of a strong business case for cloud adoption

b)   Incentive and career management aligned with evolving roles

c)   Identity and access management modes change

d)   Align KPIs with newly-enabled business capabilities

e)   Reinvent business processes to take advantage of new capabilities

Question 3

AWS CloudFront Distribution types are _____. (Select two)

a)   Horizontal

b)   Web

c)   RTMP

d)   All of the above

Question 4

To restrict any user belonging to a specific country from accessing the content, which features of AWS CloudFront use?

a)   CNAME

b)   Geo-restriction

c)   Zone apex

d)   Invalidation

Question 5

AWS CloudFront can work with the non-origin server as well. True or false?

a)   True

b)   False

Question 6

Which features of AWS CloudFront can you use to remove malicious or harmful objects before its expiration time from all edge locations?

a)   CNAME

b)   Zone Apex

c)   Invalidation

d)   Geo-restriction

Question 7

In AWS CloudFront, you can use SSL via a default URL or a custom URL. For a custom URL, you can use two types of configuration. Name them by selecting any two from the following options.

a)   Dedicated IP Custom SSL

b)   SNI Custom SSL

c)   Custom SSL using Cloudflare

d)   Custom SSL with Azure

Question 8

What are the HTTP methods thatdonot cache in CloudFront Edge Location?

a)   PUT, POST, PATCH, and DELETE

b)   PUT, POST, PATCH, and GET

c)   PUT, GET, OPTION, and DELETE

d)   HEAD, POST, PATCH, and GET

Question 9

Amazon Route 53 does not perform _____.

a)   Health checks

b)   Domain registration

c)   Load balancing

d)   DNS services

Question 10

What is the use of the Subnet Associations tab in a VPC route table?

CHAPTER 5:

Databases

The database instance includes all compute and storage attributes assigned to a database/s. It defines all components and settings of a full-fledged database environment.

Amazon AWS tenants often have multiple database instances for high availability and failover purposes assigned to a private subnet. The tenant must give a security group to a database instance. Also, the DNS hostname and DNS resolution attribute configured to resolve DNS requests.

Amazon RDS

Managed Services

It designs to provide database ready services to tenants with minimal setup. The tenant is responsible for any application-level configuration, security groups, and IAM policies. VPC security groups enable EC2 instances and RDS instances to share the same security group within a VPC. The purpose is to control access to database instances and EC2 instances inside a VPC. EC2 security groups, by contrast, control access to an EC2 model only.

Amazon installs instances, allocates capacity, and performs backups, failovers, and data replication. The tenant cannot use the SSH root directory to access the database instance.

Each database instance can contain tables created by multiple users. Amazon RDS uses Elastic Block Storage (EBS) volumes for database and logs storage.

The allocated storage can increase with various striped EBS volumes.

Read Replica

RDS enables horizontal scaling with reading replicas that allow you to scale out as database workloads increase elastically. Multiple read requests route (split) among readingimages to improve throughput and lower latency for average and peak traffic events. Adding read replicas to an RDS managed database would increase database capacity through the number of transactions per second. The effect of horizontal scaling is to distribute packets across multiple database instances. Read replicas are read-only copies that synchronize with a source (master) database instance.

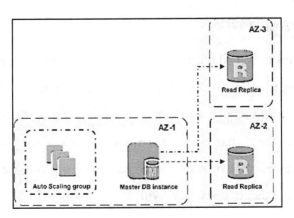

The source database is encrypted at rest and in transit for reading replications to slave databases within the Cloud. Any read replication requires selecting a target region and encryption key for the target region. You can use your passport or default key generated by KVM in the target region.

The source database sends only read-only replica updates after the initial synchronization to the slave database/s has occurred. There is currently support for up to five in-region and cross-region replicas supported per API call. Also, Amazon permits a maximum of 40 RDS database instances.

Amazon Redshift

RedShift is well suited for warehousing and analyzing Petabyte amounts of data to run SQL analytical tools. RedShift aims to provide a data warehouse solution where tenants can run sophisticated SQL queries and Business Intelligence reporting tools in real-time or offline. RedShift analysesbehaviors, patterns, and trends for gaming, stocks, logs, twitter, sensor data, and clickstreams.

Amazon Aurora

Amazon Aurora is a cost-effective open-source relational database that is fully managed by RDS. It is an enhancement to MySQL and PostgreSQL compatible RDS. It is five times faster than a standard MySQL database, has shorter recovery times, and has minimal replication latency. It provides security, fault tolerance, and durability of commercial databases at 10%.Amazon DynamoDB

Standard Features

DynamoDB is a NoSQL managed database service deployed for applications that require fast concurrent read/write lookups for smaller records with low latency (msec). Also, DynamoDB is well suited to store and retrieval of frequently accessed records. It supports multiple store models, such as documents and key-value. There is virtually unlimited scalability that adds automatically based on throughput and storage requirements.

Capacity Management

DynamoDB supports a feature called Auto Scaling that allows tenants to configure a range of capacity units with a maximum value. That enables capacity units to be increased temporarily during periods of peak traffic and prevent throttling.

DynamoDB publishes capacity metrics to CloudWatch, and any exceeded event triggers a CloudWatch alarm and SNS notification. The notice then invokes the Auto Scaling feature within DynamoDB to increase or decrease capacity units.

Amazon ElastiCache

Data Store Caching

Amazon ElastiCache is a fast in-memory caching service. It allows tenants to store frequently accessed data from multiple data stores. This strategy can reduce the processing burden to optimize data access time. The result is lower latency and response time, which speeds up queries. There is less durability, however, when compared with native database access. Amazon AWS supports the popular Memcached and Redis caching engines. It is a managed service that offloads the deployment, maintenance, and administration of caching software from tenants to the Cloud.

REVIEW QUESTIONS

Question 1:

Your new educational app for high-school students uses Amazon Cognito to handle user authentication and authorization. Now, you are thinking of adding another method of authentication and just a username and password to make the app more secure. What solution will you implement to add the extra layer of security?

(A) Add Social sign-in with Facebook, Google

(B) Add multi-factor authentication (MFA) with a Cognito user pool

(C) Add sign-in with SAML identity providers

(D) Integrate IAM with the user pool in Cognito.

Question 2:

You have hosted your new application in an Auto Scaling group of EC2 instances. Now you need to implement an SSL solution for your system to improve its security. The certificate obtains from a third-party issuer. Where can you 161 import the SSL/TLS certificate to enhance the security of your application?

(A) Amazon CloudFront

(B) AWS CloudHSM

(C) AWS Security Hub

(D) AWS Certificate Manager

Question 3:

Which of the following VPC features copies the network traffic from an elastic network interface of an Amazon EC2 instance and send the traffic to monitoring appliances?

(A) Flow logs

(B) Traffic mirroring

(C) Network access control lists (ACLs) (D) Security groups

Question 4:

Which of the following caching engines support on Amazon Elasticache? (Choose two answers)

A.   CouchBase

B.   Varnish

C.   Xcache

D.   Memcached

E.   Redis

Question 5:

Which of the following ACL rules allows inbound 38?

HTTP traffic from any IPv4 address.

(A) Rule: 100, Type: HTTP, Protocol: TCP, Port range: 80, Source: 0.0.0.0/0, Allow/Deny: ALLOW

(B) Rule: 100, Type: HTTP, Protocol: TCP, Port range: 443, Source: 0.0.0.0/0, Allow/Deny: ALLOW

(C) Rule: 100, Type: HTTP, Protocol: TCP, Port range: 53, Source: 0.0.0.0/0, Allow/Deny: ALLOW

(D) Rule: 100, Type: HTTP, Protocol: TCP, Port range: 22, Source: 0.0.0.0/0, Allow/Deny: ALLOW

Question 6:

ABC Corporation has a successful ERP web application that uses a multi-AZ RDS instance as its database tier. They are working on adding a Business Intelligence (BI) application to their offering to offer advanced reporting and analytic capabilities on their ERP data for their customers. They are worried about the additional workload from the BI application on their database tier. 95% of the BI requests will be 'read' operations on the dataset. Which of the following designs can provide BI applications with access to data without introducing a large amount of work on existing RDS instances? Which method is cost-effective?

A.   Introduce multiple 'read' replicas that replicate and sync with the primary RDS instance. The BI application will send its requests to the 'read' replicas.

B.   Introduce anElasticache layer to offload requests and cache data from the primary RDS instance. The BI application will send its recommendation to Elasticache.

C.   Introduce an Amazon EMR cluster and copy data to the EMR cluster. The BI application will send its requests to the EMR cluster.

D.   Introduce an Amazon Redshift cluster and copy data from the RDS instance using CodePipeline or DMS to keep data in sync. The BI application will send its requests to the Redshift cluster.

Question 7:

Which of the following can serve as an origin for HTTP/HTTPS CloudFront distributions? Choose three answers.

A.   Amazon load balancers

B.   Amazon S3 bucket

C.   An on-premises web server

D.   Adobe media server on EC2 instance

E.   Wowza streaming server on EC2 instance

F.   Elasticache instance

Question 8:

You are developing an application that uses Python Lambda functions. You need to store some sensitive data such as credentials for accessing the database. How will you keep this data securely and adjust your function's behavior without updating code?

(A) Use AWS Lambda environment variables (B) Use AWS Identity and Access Management (C) Use AWS CloudTrail

(D) Use AWS CodeDeploy

Question 9:

You are working for a content management company as an AWS Architect. The company needs a storage service that provides the scale and performance the content management applications require, such as high throughput and low-latency file operations. Their data needs to be stored redundantly across multiple AZs and allows concurrent connections from numerous EC2 instances hosted on multiple 60AZs. Which of the following AWS storage services is most suitable for the project?

(A) Amazon Elastic Block Store (EBS)

(B) Amazon S3

(C) AWS Storage Gateway

(D) Amazon EFS

Question 10:

You have just created a new On-Demand EC2 instance located in a subnet with ID subnet-aa181cd0 and IPv4 CIRD 172.31.16.0/20 in AWS, which hosts your WordPress blog site. The security group attached to this EC2 instance has the following inbound rules:

Inbound rules	Outbound rules	Tags			

Inbound rules					Edit inbound rules
Type	Protocol	Port range	Source	Description - optional	
HTTP	TCP	80	0.0.0.0/0	examsdigest http traffic	
Custom TCP	TCP	20 - 21	0.0.0.0/0	examsdigest ftp connection	
HTTPS	TCP	443	0.0.0.0/0	examsdigest https traffic	

You can establish an FTP connection into the EC2 instance from the internet. However, you are not able to establish an SSH connection from the internet. How to resolve the issue?

(A) In the Security Group, add an Inbound SSH rule

(B) In the Security Group, change FTP's Source IP to 172.31.16.20

(C) In the Security Group, remove the HTTPS rule

(D) In the Security Group, add an Outbound SSH rule

Question 11:

The following AWS Key Management Service practice encrypts plaintext data with a data key. Does it then encrypt the data key under another key?

(A) Key usageKey usage

(B) Envelope encryption

(C) Key spec

(D) Cryptographic operations

Question 12:

For storage of complex data types, like strings, which cache engine uses?

a)   Redis

b)   MySQL

c)   No SQL

d)   Memcached

Question 13.

Replication and Multi-AZ is one of the best approaches for

_____.

a)   Fast recovery

b)   Low latency

c)   Low availability

d)   The increasing effect of loss

Question 14:

When do you need to distribute your data over multiple nodes that the ElastiCache engine used?

a)   Members

b)   Redis

c)   Memcached

Question 15:

Which ElastiCache engine operates for the persistence of crucial stores?

a)   Members

b)   Redis

c)   Memcached

d)   MySQL

CHAPTER 6:

Analytics

I n addition to all the services and solutions discussed so far, Amazon offers services related to analytics, which help build and manage analytics solutions. Data Lakes, powered by Amazon, ensures the scalability, flexibility, and agility needed to handle more in-depth analytics, which is missing in traditional data warehouses. AWS provides analytics and machine learning services, adhering to governance and security. AWS offers a set of services to build an analytics solution and data lakes – data movement, data lake, analytics, and machine learning.

Data Movement: Import data from on-premise, real-time

One of the critical services offered by AWS is moving data from on-premise centers to the Cloud. However, there are challenges around the data movement related to bandwidth and transfer speed.

Still, AWS ensures easy transfer by providing some of the best options available. There are multiple ways to move data from the local data center to the AWS cloud

AWS Direct Connect establishes a dedicated network connection between the physical data center and Cloud.

- AWS Snowball and AWS Snowmobile use when physical entities must use to transfer massive amounts of data (PB to EB).AWS Storage Gateway to store on-premise application data directly on the Cloud.

Once data is made available for movement, Amazon ensures it can safely store in any required format so that end-users can use it for specific purposes.

AWS Glue provides the data that is made searchable and accessible for running queries by storing it in a single catalog.

- Storage: Amazon provides S3 for object storage – a scalable, securable, and durable option, specially built to store all sorts of data, from any device or application. It can keep any amount of data, without compromising retrieval speed. S3 is also famous for its compliance capabilities and security controls.

- Data Catalog: Amazon provides AWS Glue service to make data discoverable and searchable in the data lake. This managed service can extract, transform, and load data for analysis purposes. Data catalog created for data assets makes the data searchable and queryable.

- Data Archive and Backup: Amazon Glacier is the service offered by Amazon for data archival and backup. It is a secure and low-cost storage option that can use as a long-term backup and archive. It can access data in a few minutes and designtomeetthecompliance capabilities and security requirements.

Analytics and Data Warehousing

AWS provides the most effective and low-cost analytics service to analyze data stored in data lakes. These services design for various analytics purposes, such as big data processing, interactive analysis, real-time analytics, visualizations,etc.

- Big Data Processing: Amazon brings to its users Amazon EMR that helps in big data processing with the help of frameworks such as Hadoop. It is a managed service capable of processing vast data in a practical, quick, and cost-effective manner.

- Interactive analysis: Amazon Athena is another analytics service that analyzes the data stored in S3 and Glacier by running standard SQL queries. Since it is serverless, there is no infrastructure required to manage or set up this service.

- Real-time analytics: Amazon Kinesis is the service offered by Amazon for real-time analysis. It accesses, processes, and analyzes streaming data, such as application log data,

IoT data, etc., efficiently and in real-time. Therefore, the need to wait until the information is collected eliminates.

- Visualizations and dashboards: Amazon providesQuickSight for dashboards and visualizations. It is a cloud-based analytics service that helps to build great visualizations and dashboards that can use from any device or application.

- Data Warehousing: Amazon Redshift is the data warehousing service provided by Amazon to its users. It can run complex queries to analyze petabytes of data. This service includes Redshift Spectrum that runs complex queries to analyze exabytes of data stored in S3.

We read about data lakes, but do we know how lakes form?

AWS Lake Formation is an Amazon service that helps in setting up a data lake, which is a secure and centralized repository to hold data in its original form but prepared for analysis. A data lake breaks silos by combining different types of analytics, gaining better and deeper insights into the data.

Creating and managing a data lake is time-consuming and complicated because it involves extracting data from different sources, monitoring this data stream, collecting the keys on this data, defining transformations, etc.

The users can then utilize the centralized data catalog that holds the relevant data for analysis. Now that we know how these lakes are created most thoroughly with the help of Lake Formation let us conclude its benefits –

1. It helps build the data lakes in no time. With the help of the Lake Formation service, data can be moved, stored, cataloged, and set up in no time. All you need to provide to this service are the data sources and the security controls required for this data. Lake Formation then crawls over this data and moves it to the newly created data lake on Amazon S3

2. Lake Formation service simplifies security management as per the security controls defined by the user. It leverages to define the governance and security policies centrally and then apply them to analyze the applications. These policies implement across the services without configuring them manually across other services, such as IAM, Key Management Service, etc. It eliminates the effort required in configuring the security policies across different services.

3. Lake Formation service enables the users to self-access the data stored in the lakes. The user creates the data catalog that holds data sets available to users and groups of users. It helps the users quickly find the right data for

their specific needs. Records also ensure secured access to the data and make it easy for analysts to analyze it.

Predictive Analytics

To perform predictive analytics, AWS offers various machine learning services and tools to run on AWS data lakes.

- Platform Services: Amazon SageMaker is a platform service offered by Amazon to build, train, and deploy machine learning models. It provides everything that is needed to connect to the training data, to select and optimize the algorithms, and to deploy auto-scaling clusters of EC2.

- Application Services: For all those looking for a pre-built AI functionality in their applications, Amazon provides APIs for natural language processing. These services enable the developers to add an element of intelligence into their applications without building their models.

REVIEW QUESTIONS

Question 1

You are the solution architect for a national retail chain having stores in major cities. Each store uses an on-premise application for the sales transaction. At the end of the day at 11 pm, data from each store should upload to Amazon storage, which will be more than 30TB of data; the data then should be processed in Hadoop and the results stored in the data warehouse. What combination of AWS services will you use?

1.   Amazon Data Pipeline, Amazon S3, Amazon EMR, Amazon DynamoDB

2.   Amazon Data Pipeline, Amazon Elastic Block Storage, Amazon S3, Amazon EMR, Amazon Redshift

3.   Amazon Data Pipeline, Amazon S3, Amazon EMR, Amazon Redshift

4.   Amazon Data Pipeline, Amazon Kinesis, Amazon S3, Amazon EMR, Amazon Redshift, Amazon EC2

Question 2

You are running a media-rich website with a global audience from us-east-1 for a customer in the publishing industry. The website updates every 20 minutes. The web-tier of the site sits on three EC2 instances inside an Auto Scaling Group. The Auto Scaling group configures to scale when CPU utilization of the cases is greater than 70%. The Auto Scaling group sits behind an Elastic Load Balancer. Your static content lives in S3 and is distributed globally by CloudFront. Your RDS database is already the largest instance size available. CloudWatch metrics show that your RDS instance usually has around 2GB of memory free and an average CPU utilization of 75%. Currently, it is taking your users in Japan and Australia approximately 3 - 5 seconds to load your website, and you have to ask to help reduce these load-times. How might you improve your page load times? [Select 3]

A) Setup CloudFront with dynamic content support to enable the caching of re-usable content from the media-rich website.

B) Set up a clone of your production environment in the Asia Pacific region and configure latency-based routing on Route 53.

C) Increase the Provisioned IOPS on the EBS Volume.

D) Change your Auto Scaling Group to scale when CPU Utilization is only 50%, rather than 70%.

E) Use ElastiCache to cache the most commonly accessed DB queries

Question 3

A customer has enabled website hosting on a bucket named "devtoolslogging" in the Singapore region. What website URL assigns to your bucket?

A) devtoolslogging.s3-website-ap-southeast-1.amazonaws.com

B) s3-website.devtoolslogging.amazonaws.com

C) s3-website.devtoolslogging.website-ap-southeast-1.amazonaws.com

D) devtoolslogging.ap-southeast-1.amazonaws.com

Question 4

A company does not want to manage their databases. Which of the following services altogethercontainsdatabases provided by AWS?

A) AWS RDS

B) DynamoDB

C) Oracle RDS

D) Elastic Map Reduce

Question 5

Your company has recently migrated the on-premise application to AWS and deploying them in VPCs. As part of the proactive monitoring and audit purpose, they want to continuously analyze the Cloudtrail event logs to collect different operational metrics in real-time. For example:

• Total calls by IP, service, API call, IAM user

• Amazon EC2 API failures (or any other service)

• Anomalous behavior of Amazon EC2 API (or any other use)

• Top 10 API calls across all services

Which AWS services will you use?

1. S3, Kinesis Data Analytics, Lambda, DynamoDB

2. EC2, S3, Kinesis Data Analytics, DynamoDB

3. EC2, S3, Kinesis Data Analytics, Lambda, DynamoDB

4. Kinesis Data Firehose, S3, Kinesis Data Analytics, Lambda, DynamoDB

Question 6

Which of the following functions of the EMR HDFS file system?Choose 4.

1. It is a distributed, scalable, and portable file system for Hadoop.

2.   It allows clusters to store data in Amazon S3.

3.   Instance store and EBS volume storage area used for HDFS data.

4.   Amazon EBS volumes attached to EMR clusters are ephemeral: the works delete upon set and instance termination.

5.   HDFS is a common choice for persistent collections.

6.   HDFS is a common choice for transient clusters.

Question 7

Which AWS service you will use for business analytics dashboards and visualizations?

1.   Amazon Athena

2.   Amazon EMR

3.   Amazon Elasticsearch Service

4.   Amazon QuickSight

Question 8

You have a database-style application that frequently has multiple reads and writes across the data set. Which of the following AWS storage services can host this application? [Select 2]

A) Elastic File Service (EFS)

B) Glacier

C) S3

D) EBS

Question 9

Which AWS database service will you choose for Online Analytical Processing (OLAP)?

1.   Amazon RDS

2.   Amazon Redshift

3.   Amazon Glacier

4.   Amazon DynamoDB

Question 10

Which of the following AWS services can you leverage to analyze logs for customer-facing applications and websites? Choose 2.

1.   Amazon S3

2.   Amazon Elasticsearch

3.   Amazon Athena

4.   Amazon Cloudwatch

CHAPTER 7:

Application Integration

Amazon SQS

SQS is a distributed message queuing system

- it allows you to decouple components of an application system, so they are independent.
- Ex: An EC2 Instance fails
- Another EC2 will pick it up, and
- The message will stay in the SQS queue.
- Pull based (not pushed)
- Standard Queues:
- Is the Default SQS setting
- Best effort ordering
- Message delivered at least once
- Visibility Timeout:
- The default is 30 seconds.

Amazon SNS

- Amazon SNS, Simple Notification Service, sends notifications from the Cloud.
- SNS is:
- Highly scalable
- Flexible
- Cost-effective
- Important in production systems
- SNS delivers messages to:
- Mobile devices
- SMS text
- Email
- SQS
- HTTP endpoints
- Trigger Lambda functions

AmazonSWF

Amazon Simple Workflow Service coordinates works across distributed application components

- SWF can run on:
- EC2 Instances
- Machines behind firewalls
- Amazon Cloud infrastructure

- SWF maximum retention period for a workflow is up to 1 year

- Always measured in seconds

REVIEW QUESTIONS

Question 1:

A company hosts a multiplayer game on AWS. The application uses Amazon EC2 instances in a single Availability Zone, and users connect over Layer 4. Solutions Architect has been tasked with making the architecture highly available and also more cost-effective.

How can the solutions architect best meet these requirements? (Select TWO)

1: Configure an Auto Scaling group to add or remove instances in the Availability Zone automatically

2: Increase the number of cases and use smaller EC2 instance types

3: Configure a Network Load Balancer in front of the EC2 instances

4: Configure an Application Load Balancer in front of the EC2 instances

5: Configure an Auto Scaling group to add or remove samples in multiple Availability Zones automatically

Question 2:

A solutions architect is designing the infrastructure to run an application on Amazon EC2 instances. The application requires high availability and must dynamically scale based on demand to be cost-efficient.

What should the solutions architect do to meet these requirements?

1: Configure an Application Load Balancer in front of an Auto Scaling group to deploy instances to multiple Regions

2: Configure an Amazon CloudFront distribution in front of an Auto Scaling group to deploy models to multiple Regions

3: Configure an Application Load Balancer in front of an Auto Scaling group to deploy instances to multiple Availability Zones

4: Configure an Amazon API Gateway API in front of an Auto Scaling group to deploy models to multiple Availability Zones

Question 3:

An application that runs a computational fluid dynamics workload uses a tightly-coupled HPC architecture that uses the MPI protocol and runs across many nodes.

A service-managed deployment is required to minimize operational overhead.

Which deployment option is MOST suitable for provisioning and managing the resources required for this use case?

1: Use Amazon EC2 Auto Scaling to deploy instances in multiple subnets

2: Use AWS CloudFormation to deploy a Cluster Placement Group on EC2

3: Use AWS Batch to deploy a multi-node parallel job

4: Use AWS Elastic Beanstalk to provision and manage the EC2 instances

Question 4:

A security officer requires that access to company financial reports logs. The word stores in an Amazon S3 bucket. Additionally, any modifications to the log files must be detected.

Which actions should a solutions architect take?

1: Use S3 server access logging on the bucket that houses the reports with the read and write data events and the log file validation options enabled

2: Use S3 server access logging on the bucket that houses the pieces with the read and corresponds management events, and log file validation options enabled

3: Use AWS CloudTrail to create a new trail. Configure the path to log read and write data events on the S3 bucket that houses the reports. Log these events to a unique bucket, and enable log file validation

4: Use AWS CloudTrail to create a new trail. Configure the path to log read and write management events on the S3 bucket that houses the reports. Log these events to a unique bucket, and enable log file validation

Question 5:

An application runs on Amazon EC2 Linux instances. The application generates log files that write using standard API calls. A storage solution requires that it can be used to store the files indefinitely and must allow concurrent access to all files. Which storage service meets these requirements, and is the MOST cost-effective?

1: Amazon EBS

2: Amazon EFS

3: Amazon EC2 instance store

4: Amazon S3

Question 6:

A company has some statistical data stored in an Amazon RDS database. The company wants to allow users to access this information using an API. A solutions architect must create a solution that helps sporadic access to the data, ranging from no requests to large bursts of traffic. Which solution should the solutions architect suggest?

1: Set up an Amazon API Gateway and use Amazon ECS

2: Set up an Amazon API Gateway and use AWS Elastic Beanstalk

3: Set up an Amazon API Gateway and use AWS Lambda functions

4: Set up an Amazon API Gateway and use Amazon EC2 with Auto Scaling

Question 7:

A web application in a three-tier architecture runs on a fleet of Amazon EC2 instances. Performance issues reports and investigations point to insufficient swap space. The operations team requires monitoring to determine if this is correct.

What should a solutions architect recommend?

1: Configure an Amazon CloudWatch SwapUsage metric dimension. Monitor the SwapUsageextent in the EC2 metrics in CloudWatch

2: Use EC2 metadata to collect information, then publish it to Amazon CloudWatch custom metrics. Monitor SwapUsage metrics in CloudWatch

3: Install an Amazon CloudWatch agent on the instances. Run an appropriate script on a set schedule. Monitor SwapUtilization metrics in CloudWatch

4: Enable detailed monitoring in the EC2 console. Create an Amazon CloudWatch SwapUtilization custom metric. Monitor SwapUtilization metrics in CloudWatch

Question 8:

A gaming company collects real-time data and stores it in an on-premises database system. The company is migrating to AWS and needs better performance for the database. A solutions architect has asked to recommend an in-memory database that supports data replication.

Which database should a solutions architect recommend?

1: Amazon RDS for MySQL

2: Amazon RDS for PostgreSQL

3: Amazon ElastiCache for Redis

4: Amazon ElastiCache for Memcached

Question 9:

To increase performance and redundancy for an application, a company has decided to run multiple implementations in different AWS Regions behind network load balancers. The company currently advertises the application using two public IP addresses from separate /24 address ranges and would prefer not to change these.

Which actions should a solutions architect take? (Select TWO)

1: Create an Amazon Route 53 geolocation-based routing policy

2: Create an AWS Global Accelerator and attach endpoints in each AWS Region

3: Assign new static anycast IP addresses and modify any existing pointers

4: Migrate both public IP addresses to the AWS Global Accelerator

5: Create PTR records to map currentlyavailable IP addresses to an Alias

Question 10:

A highly elastic application consists of three tiers. The application tier runs in an Auto Scaling group and processes data and writes it to an Amazon RDS MySQL database. The Solutions Architect wants to restrict access to the database tier to accept traffic from the instances in the application tier.

How can the Solutions Architect configure secure access to the database tier?

1: Configure the database security group to allow traffic only from the application security group

2: Configure the database security group to allow traffic only from port 3306

3: Configure a Network ACL on the database subnet to deny all traffic to ports other than 3306

4: Configure a Network ACL on the database subnet to allow all traffic from the application subnet

Question 11:

A website runs on a Microsoft Windows server in an on-premises data center. The web server is being migrated to Amazon EC2 Windows instances in multiple Availability Zones on AWS. The web server currently uses data stored in on-premises network-attached storage (NAS) device.

Which replacement to the NAS file share is MOST resilient and durable?

1: Migrate the file share to Amazon EBS

2: Migrate the file share to AWS Storage Gateway

3: Migrate the file share to Amazon FSx for Windows File Server

4: Migrate the file share to Amazon Elastic File System (Amazon EFS)

Question 12:

An application monitored using Amazon GuardDuty. A Solutions Architect needs to be notified by email of medium to high severity events. How can this be achieved?

1: Configure an Amazon CloudWatch alarm that triggers based on a GuardDuty metric

2: Create an Amazon CloudWatch Events rule that triggers an Amazon SNS topic

3: Create an Amazon CloudWatch Logs rule that triggers an AWS Lambda function

4: Configure an Amazon CloudTrail alarm the triggers based on GuardDuty API activity

Question 13:

A solutions architect is creating a document submission application for a school. The application will use an Amazon S3 bucket for storage. The solution must prevent the accidental deletion of the documents and ensure that all versions of the papers are available. Users must be able to upload and modify the copies.

Which combination of actions should it take to meet these requirements? (Select TWO)

1: Set read-only permissions on the bucket

2: Enable versioning on the bucket

3: Attach an IAM policy to the bucket

4: Enable MFA Delete on the bucket

5: Encrypt the bucket using AWS SSE-S3

Question 14:

An HR application stores employment records on Amazon S3. Regulations mandate the forms retains for seven years. Once created, the records are accessed infrequently for the first three months and then must be available within 10 minutes if required after that.

Which lifecycle action meets the requirements while MINIMIZING cost?

1: Store the data in S3 Standard for three months, then transition to S3 Glacier

2: Store the data in S3 Standard-IA for three months, then transition to S3 Glacier

3: Store the data in S3 Standard for three months, then transition to S3 Standard-IA

4: Store the data in S3 Intelligent Tiering for three months, then transition to S3 Standard-IA

Question 15:

An application calls to a REST API running on Amazon EC2 instances behind an Application Load Balancer (ALB). Most API calls complete quickly. What steps can a Solutions Architect take to minimize the effects of the long-running API calls?

1: Change the EC2 instance to one with enhanced networking to reduce latency

2: Create an Amazon SQS queue and decouple the long-running API calls

3: Increase the ALB idle timeout to allow the long-running requests to complete

4: Change the ALB to a Network Load Balancer (NLB) and use SSL/TLS termination

Question 16:

A company is deploying an Amazon ElastiCache for Redis cluster. Enhance security, and a password should be required to access the database. What should the solutions architect use?

1: AWS Directory Service

2: AWS IAM Policy

3: Redis AUTH command

4: VPC Security Group

CHAPTER 8:

AWS Security, Identity & Compliance

G eneral Security practices are essential from an architect's perspective for the exam.

AWS CloudTrail

It is an essential service from a security perspective. The AWS CloudTrail service can use to monitor all API activity from the AWS account. Whether you are issuing API calls either from the SDK or PowerShell or using the console, everything will record in the AWS CloudTrail service.

· It's also perfect when you want to ensure compliance for your company.

· Also, if you suspect any malicious activity in your account, you can check the CloudTrail logs to see if any irregular API activities have fires. Some resources span up, which is not supposed to create; you can see for this API calls in the CloudTrail logs.

· As an architect, you should always enable CloudTrail logs for all regions. It also ensures that if any future parts get created by AWS, they automatically get covered.

IAM

When you are creating IAM users, ensure to give them access based on 'least privilege.' In other words, ensure that you give them permissions based on only the tasks they are going to do.

· Use multi-factor authentication wherever possible.

· Change the password policy; don't keep the default password policy. In the past system, you can mention the characters to be specified when creating the password and how long the password should last (the password).

· Disable the root access keys.

Buckets in S3

For the buckets in S3, you have the bucket policy, which can use to manage the access via the underlying objects. Even when you're giving access to external AWS accounts, remember that you can do this via the bucket policy.

The pre-signed URLs enables you to give a time limit for when a user can access an object.

IAM Roles

IAM roles use for secure access to your resources. Let's say you have an application on an EC2 instance that needs to access a service like S3 or DynamoDB and attach an IAM Role to that instance with the specific privilege.

It' so use access keys, but w during development time, when you go onto deployment or production, ensure that you use IAM Roles for secure access.

Even if you are using a lambda function to access an external resource like DynamoDB or S3, ensure that an IAM Role is attached to the lambda function.

Network Security

If you want an instance in a private subnet to access public resources like DynamoDB, S3, or KMS, remember you can't use the NAT gateway. You then have to use a unique feature known as VPC Endpoints. There are two types of VPC Endpoints:

VPC Gateway Endpoints: This uses when you want to access either S3 or DynamoDB.

VPC Interface Endpoint: This uses when you want to access other services such as KMS.

What you do is that you create a VPC endpoint to your service, attach it to the VPC, and then you can make your instance in the private subnet access that resource via the endpoint.

For Redshift, if you want the data during the LOAD or COPY process to be private (that is, it should not go via the internet) via a VPC, you can enable one feature known as Redshift Enhance VPC Routing. If you want to monitor IP addresses of traffic into your VPC, use VPC Flow Logs.

Use Bastion host if an administrator needs to administer instances in your private subnet. The bastion host will kill in the public subnet; ensure the right security groups are in place only to allow access to the administrator's workstation.

REVIEW QUESTIONS

Question 1

Amazon Cognito means

Question 2:

When applying the security best practices, how should your team members access resources in the AWS account?

Question 3:

What should AWS do to prevent customers from using an unsustainable part of available resources?

Question 4:

How can you describe the cloud service model known as infrastructure as a service?

Question 5:

What method of authentication would you need to access your files remotely using the CLI?

Question 6:

What description can you give the method of protecting your data locally on-site, in transit, and during storage on the AWS cloud platform?

Question 7:

What is the full file size allowed in Amazon S3?

1.   5 terabytes

2.   0 bytes

3.   5 gigabytes

4.   Unlimited

Question 8:

What is the significant advantage of using resource tags with your assets on Amazon Web Services?

Question 9:

An application running on an Amazon ECS container instance using the EC2 launch type needs permission to write data to Amazon DynamoDB.

How can you assign these permissions only to the specific ECS task that is running the application?

1: Create an IAM policy with permissions to DynamoDB and attach it to the container instance

2: Create an IAM policy with permissions to DynamoDB and assign It to a task using the taskRoleArn parameter

3: Use a security group to allow outbound connections to DynamoDB and give it to the container instance

4: Modify the AmazonECSTaskExecutionRolePolicy policy to add permissions for DynamoDB

Question 10:

The solution architect is designing a new workload, in which AWS Lambda functions will access Amazon DynamoDB tables.

What are the MOST secure means of granting the Lambda function access to the DynamoDB table?

1: Create an identity and access management (IAM) role with the required permissions to access DynamoDB tables, and assign parts to Lambda functions

2: Create a DynamoDB username and password and give them to the Developer to use in the Lambda function

3: Create an identity and access management (IAM) role allowing access from AWS Lambda and assign the part to the DynamoDB table

CHAPTER 9:

Network Architectures

These objectives are selecting high-performing network solutions and designing cost-optimized network architectures for your workload. You can get some questions on the use case scenario of high-performing networking solutions in the exam, so you need to understand these concepts in detail. Let's try to figure out what could ask in the examination.

When considering Network Architectures, there are three types of network solutions for your workload. They are flat network architectures, segmented network architectures, and hybrid connectivity. Let's discuss flat network architectures first. So, in the flat network architecture, you have a single VPC architecture, which means a single account in an available VPC. Itis how Virtual Private Cloud develops; you select a CIDR for a VPC and split it into subnets and individual availability zones. Then the subnets are placed into routing tables where they subdivide into Public and Private Subnets. You can have five CIDR blocks attached to one VPC.

So in single VPC architecture, limited data transfer is considered unless you have dependencies that reach AZ boundaries. You can even have more than 300,000 IP addresses so your workloads can start to scale. And you can also split native constructs into Subnets Route Tables, NACLs, and Security Groups. So if you have a VPC architecture in which you can have several hyper-scale customers who can operate hundreds of thousands of services like microservices within a single account in an available VPC, then the network architecture suitable for you is single VPC architecture.

Let's say you have a single VPC that's Multi-Tenant, and then you need to ensure that one of these tenants does not consume all your resources and not sharing with other users. So it can get rather challenging to have everyone in the same bucket when you talk of cost allocation or policy enforcement. Thus, VPC Sharing is the ideal approach to use a single VPC with multiple accounts. It uses the Amazon Resource Access Manager to share your subnets and resources with other charges in your AWS organization like the Transit Gateway, Route 53, and Resolving Rules within your VPC.

So in the single VPC multiple accounts or shared VPC model, you share a subnet to participants. Then they may launch their resources like EC2 instances or databases or ELBs within these subnets that you own. It is essential from the exam perspective. VPC sharing has account-specific cost allocation, a single VPC blast radius, and shared DNS. Still, there is limited access control for application owners. Policy control and isolation that the individual AWS account provides can implement on that the single VPC layer. This method of centralizing and reusing VPC components reduce costs for the management and maintenance of your environment.

Ideally, when users look at these designs, they seek to optimize the costs. That's why they place them into one single VPC because they have a lot of dependencies between workloads. Thus, users don't require mediums like the Transit Gateway, VPC peering, and private link for the VPC management with one single VPC. Let's move onto the segmented network architecture.

In Segmented network architecture, we have multiple accounts in multiple VPCs. So, this architecture prefers for large companies that can control and push beyond the AWS account limits. So this architecture is required when users want isolation between their dev tests and production workloads or want to isolate their business unit and workload category.

And another reason that it designs to isolate the individual microservices completely. For example, if you have a PCI or HIPAA compliance workload, then you can use it, or to simply separate the software testing and production environments. You can also isolate your blast radius if your workload crosses the VPC and the account boundaries. It provides you with the distributed service limitations that you can use to scale on AWS.

This approach increases the complexity of IP management, like what type of IP range or CIDR do I assign for a bunch of my VPCs? How can I communicate with lots of other VPCs? You also need to consider how you handle access control between resources across different VPCs and IAM and networking accounts.

So here come several patterns of VPC networking connectivity. First, we have VPC Peering. Let's say you wanted to connect all your VPCs. In this case, you use VPC Peering to create a complete communication network between the VPCs. VPC Peering is easy to set up and has no bandwidth limitations. VPC Peering can enable for VPCs between the same regions, across regions, or between different accounts. But, let's say you have four VPCs, so you need to set up six peering links with the four VPCs and approve and configure routing for each of them. It could ask in the examination.

If you want to manage multiple networks and infrastructures, you can use Transit Gateway for that purpose. When you have hundreds of VPCs and connections, Transit Gateway eliminates the time-consuming process of linking individual VPCs with each other through VPC peering and creating VPN tunnels between the on-premise and each VPC to allow on-premise connectivity. It uses either a VPN connection or Direct Connect connection. It's like you try to merge your edge connectivity with AWS. By default, it can scale up to 5,000 VPCs and supports equal-cost multi-path VPNs.

Moreover, it also allows you to route flexibly and provides you with multiple routing tables. You must understand the difference between VPC peering and Transit Gateway from an exam perspective.Let's see the concept of PrivateLink, which is very important for the exam. Now every application needs to communicate with one another through three-way TCP handshakes. So PrivateLink is specially built for traditional TCP client-server relation where you have a client on one side. A server lives in a different VPC. You create a hole in another VPC to provide services on a specific port and an IP address to another VPC.It is different from the VPC Peering and Transit Gateway since it punishes a hole for that service. It does not provide two-way connectivity for the entire VPC's. It uses because it entirely reduces the visibility to and from shared services. It also supports IAM policy on the endpoint itself, and it solves large and complex network address translation.

Let's consider a use case in which you use PrivateLink to access dependencies on-premise with overlapping IPs. In this architecture, you have on-premise services, and you have cloud-based services and want to share these resources. One option is to use a mediator or NAT VPC in this model because it allows you to set up bi-directional private links to expose endpoints in the cloud and on-premise. These are a virtual interface that you are not targeting, like a single server or a load balancer on-prem.

Therefore, the IP address of your client in the VPC is 10.0.1.15, and your local server has the same IP address. Therefore, here you put PrivateLink into the client's VPC. You have a network load balancer in the mediator or NAT VPC. Its IP target passes to the local database server through a direct connection... When the server receives the request, the request comes from the IP address of the mediator.

The reverse is that I have a private link in the mediator or NAT VPC, and I expose my service via a personalconnection in the NLB within the VPC itself. The same IP addresses of the client-server solve the NAT issue, as I mentioned earlier. You can see the difference in the diagram below:

Now how can you use PrivateLink for cost optimization? Thus, Centralizing interface VPC endpoint is one of the best ways of deploying PrivateLink to optimize costs. Some customers choose to host private link endpoints in shared services VPC because it reduces the cost of AWS PrivateLink endpoints based on the traffic profile. But you may end up paying for the data transfer costs when you have a Kinesis endpoint or something that uses a lot of bandwidth. Then you would just host the endpoint yourself.

Another thing to consider in this situation is when you create a PrivateLink; the service creates a private hosted zone for you. The PrivateLink service owns this personal hosted zone. You don't own it, so you can't connect it to other VPCs. Therefore, the privately hosted endpoints outside the VPC cannot be attached. Data processing costs can also increase according to how consumers communicate with a centralized endpoint. Thus, if you want to reduce costs and private link endpoints, that might be a good option for you.

Now, let's see the hybrid connectivity models that you need to know generally for the exam. First is AWS Site-to-Site VPN connectivity. The first option is to terminate the site-to-site VPN connection on a Transit Gateway. And then, Transit Gateway spreads connectivity to thousands of VPCs. The second model involves completing your Site-to-Site VPN connection on a Virtual Private Gateway attached to a single VPC. The third option is to terminate the VPN on an EC2 instance that runs VPN software from the AWS marketplace. You should choose to use the Transit Gateway for your VPN termination because it simplifies management by reducing the number of VPN tunnels and BGP sessions to handle. And it also scales horizontally in terms of throughput and the scale of the number of VPCs.

While VPN is an excellent option to start up, but may not be ideal for some production traffic. Therefore, choose AWS direct connect, which gives high bandwidth connectivity between your data center and the AWS. It is all from hybrid connectivity that could ask in the examination.

Let's discuss some of the differences between AWS Global Accelerator and CloudFront, which is very important from the exam perspective. Both offer you the AWS backbone network to decrease latency for end-users. So if you have a website that is deployed just to one region, use CloudFront. It will also give you the capability of Response Caching and Lambda Edges. In Response Caching, you can cache static assets or full pages of your website close to end-users, which is very handy. And Lambda edge allows you to execute small pieces of software in a region close to the user in edge location. Due to this reason, CloudFront is a better option for minimizing latency for end-users. Still, then, Global Accelerator offers you two public IPs, and because of that, it can work with any DNS system.

And in terms of failover between regions, the global accelerator is best because it offers you Multi-region failover. So, in case your website is deployed in more than one area. It's good to use CloudFront and Global Accelerator to deliver content to end-users and split traffic between sites.

In case you use API, which would never need caching, then a global accelerator is aright choice because caching is not required. Global accelerators can distribute content and distribute API responses to end-users, and also, it can switch traffic between regions. It also distributes traffic between multiple areas. Another feature of Global Accelerator is that its IP addressresolves regionally.

Conclusion

Amazon continues to roll out new regional places, so you're most likely to have access to a neighboring service location and the abundant AWS ecosystem.

AWS Is the Leading Cloud-Computing Provider. AWS is exceptionally popular. However, its popularity has the impact of making the service much better. Today, Amazon has an enhancing cycle taking place:

- Having more users produces a higher volume of usage, which increases the amount of hardware Amazon purchases, which reduces its costs utilizing economies of scale, which hands down to users in the type of lower prices.

-Because of the large number of users, companies that use complimentary services (online application integration, for example) decide to initially put their services in AWS, making the total service much better, which draws in more users.

Everywhere you turn, the word development is a hot subject. Individuals acknowledge that innovation makes life much better and can improve the future for generations to come.

AWS has changed how technology provides to clients and, as a result, has enabled a surge of development. The development and low cost related to AWS permit little and big businesses to rapidly and cheaply introduce brand-new offerings as one development consultant put it:

AWS has decreased the cost of failure. AWS lets you quickly check out a brand-new item to see whether it "gets traction." Moreover, if a new offering gets traction and starts to accelerate, AWS lets you quickly scale it. On the other hand, if the service does not attain adoption, that's no issue-- the ease of shutting down AWS resources means that very little is lost if an ingenious perspective offering does not turn out.".

I forecast that a lot more innovation will happen as more individuals and companies become knowledgeable about AWS and its capabilities. AWS will be to the details.

AWS Is Cost Effective.

Much of that expense reduction is because of AWS: its on-demand low prices and simple termination without any charges make it possible to utilize and spend precisely as much computing capacity as you require when you require it.

The expense effectiveness of AWS isn't limited to start-ups, though. Every company can take advantage of access to inexpensive computing that doesn't need a prolonged commitment. It's a sign of the significantbenefits of AWS that much.

When there, the existing supplier community is terrified of what will occur.

Customers begin to demand AWS-like prices and benefit from them.

Amazon is a different company. Unlike many companies that strive to raise their own earnings margins, Amazon passes on the advantages of energy at lower costs. There's no factor to anticipate that this method will change.

Amazon can make your IT dollars go further if you're a part of any company, little or big. It's substantially more expense significant than the conventional mode of acquiring IT resources: large up-front payments with little certainty about whether the amount provisioned is too small (or too much).

AWS Aligns Your Organization.

In the 1980s, the increase of networked PCs (the client-server architecture) transformed mainframes into a traditional environment-- and led to Microsoft ending up being the dominant gamer in the software market. In the 1990s, the Internet made the Web (and HTTP process) the de facto architecture for all applications-and, led to the domination of businesses such as Google and, of course, Amazon.Cloud computing is the next-generation platform for computing. Its characteristics of highly scalable, on-demand computing services that are readily available within minutes and bring no requirement for long-lasting dedication will end up being the foundation for all future applications. As the saying goes, resistance is futile.

Its record of innovation and rate competitiveness is unrivaled in the market. I forecast that ten years from now, AWS will be the Microsoft or Google of its period. Your organization should become knowledgeable about AWS and determine how to utilize it successfully-- otherwise. It may discover the IT equivalent of a buggy whip maker after Henry Ford developed the assembly line.

AWS Is Good for Your Career.

The great business is to be the best individual at the right time and in the best place. To be the best person is all you have-your ability to work, productive working relationships, and wisdom. No matter which field or function you operate, these attributes will help you succeed.

However, remaining in the ideal place at the perfect time has a lot to do with insight about where a brand-new market, made possible by some development, is emerging and planting your flag there.

In the 1920s, or entered TV services in the 1950s, or the Internet in the 1990s, as new markets sought expertise to build great companies, people entering the automotive industry experienced tremendous opportunities.

Technology innovation produces powerful abilities gaps in the market and makes those with understanding and experience necessary. Suppose you think that AWS is. The next-generation platform, too, can represent "the best place at the time" for you.

Answers to Review Questions

Computer Answers

Question 1 Answer: 1

One is correct. The best way to achieve this is to use an event notification on the S3 bucket that triggers a function that runs the code.

Two are incorrect. Lambda does not poll S3.

Three is incorrect. You would not use Amazon SNS in this scenario as it is an unnecessary additional step.

Question 2 Answer(s): 3

One is incorrect. EFS is a file-based storage system that is accessed using the NFS protocol.

Two are incorrect. EBS is a block-based storage system for mounting volumes.

Three is correct. Amazon S3 is an object-based storage system that uses standards-based REST web interfaces to work with objects.

Four are incorrect. Amazon FSx for Windows File Server provides a fully managed Microsoft filesystem that is mounted using SMB.

Question 3 Answer(s): 4

One is incorrect. Reserved instances require a commitment over 1 or 3 years.

Twoare incorrect. Spot instances are suitable for cost-sensitive workloads that can afford to be interrupted. This workload must complete, so Spot instances would not be ideal.

Three is incorrect. Dedicated Instances are Amazon EC2 instances that run in a VPC on hardware dedicated to a single customer. It would be more expensive, and there is no need for dedicated hardware in this case.

Fourare correct. On-demand instances are ideal for short-term or unpredictable workloads. You don't get a discount, but you do have more flexibility with no commitments.

Question 4 Answer(s): 2

One is incorrect. You cannot nest buckets (create buckets inside other buckets).

Two is correct. You can mimic the hierarchy of a filesystem by creating a folder in your buckets.

Three is incorrect. You cannot upload objects within other objects.

Fourare incorrect. Tiering your data is done for performance, not to mimic a filesystem.

Question 5 Answer(s): 4

One is incorrect. Aurora Global Database spans multiple regions for disaster recovery.

Twoare incorrect. Aurora Replicas scales read operations but do not allow writes to multiple DB instances.

Three is incorrect. Aurora Cross-Region Replicase scale read operations across regions. They do not allow writes to DB instances in multiple AZs.

Fourare correct. Amazon Aurora Multi-Master adds the ability to scale out write performance across multiple Availability Zones and provides configurable read after write consistency.

Question 6 Answer(s): 1

One is correct. DynamoDB is a schema-less NoSQL database that provides push-button scaling.

Twoare incorrect. ElastiCache is an in-memory relational database, so it is not schema-less.

Three is incorrect. Amazon RDS is a relational database (not schema-less) and uses EC2 instancesnot to offer push-button scaling.

Fourare incorrect. Amazon Aurora is a relational database (not schema-less) and uses EC2 instances not to offer push-button scaling.

Question 7 Answer(s): 3

One is incorrect. DynamoDB Global Tables provides a multi-region, multi-master database solution.

Twoare incorrect. DynamoDB Auto Scaling is for scaling read and write capacity.

Three is correct. DynamoDB Streams maintains a list of item level changes and can integrate with Lambda to create triggers.

Fourare incorrect. DynamoDB DAX provides microsecond latency for reading requests to DynamoDB tables.

Question 8 Answer(s):2

One is incorrect. RedShift is not a schema-less database; it is a relational database.

Two is correct. RedShift is a data warehouse optimized for online analytics processing (OLAP).

Three is incorrect. RedShift optimizes online analytics processing (OLAP) use cases, not online transactional processing (OLTP) use cases.

Fourare incorrect. RedShift can be analyzed using SQL, not Hadoop (should use EMR).

Question 9 Answer(s): 1

One is correct. Redis provides data persistence.

Twoare incorrect. Memcached does not provide data persistence.

Question 10 Answer(s): 4

One is incorrect. You do not attach Internet gateways to subnets.

Twoare incorrect. You do not attach Internet gateways to subnets.

Three is incorrect. You do not attach Internet gateways to AZs.

Fourare correct. Internet Gateways are attached to the VPC.

Question 11 Answer(s): 2

One is incorrect. VPCs are not global.

Two is correct. VPC is regional and can create a VPC in each region.

Three is incorrect. An availability zone exists within a region, and a VPC can span subnets attached to all AZs in the area.

Question 12 Answer(s): 4

One is incorrect. An MX record is a mail exchange record for email servers.Twoare incorrect. A record simply points a name to an IP address.Three is incorrect. A CNAME record cannot points at a domain apex record like dctlabs.com.

Fourare correct. An Alias record can be used with domain apex records and can point to an ELB.

Question 13 Answer(s): 1

One is correct. The ALB only supports layer seven, which is HTTP and HTTPS – not TCP.

Twoare incorrect. This is the correct combination of listener/protocol.

Three is incorrect. This is the correct combination of listener/protocol.

Question 14 Answer(s):2

One is incorrect. EC2 Auto Scaling is not an example of vertical scaling.

Two is correct. EC2 Auto Scaling scales horizontally by launching or terminating EC2 instances.

Question 15 Answer(s):3

One is incorrect. AWS Managed VPN uses the public Internet, so it's not considered a private connection or low-latency.

Twoare incorrect. AWS VPN CloudHub uses for creating a hub and spoke topology of VPN connections. Use the public Internet, not personal relationships.

Three is correct. AWS Direct Connect uses private network connections into the AWS Cloud and is high-bandwidth and low-latency. It is suitable for establishing hybrid cloud configurations.

Fourare incorrect. A Transit VPC uses for connecting VPCs across regions.

Question 16 Answer(s):3

One is incorrect. Route 53 latency based routing does not provide automatic failover or 2 IP addresses.

Twoare incorrect. Amazon CloudFront is a content delivery network. It does not perform automatic routing across regions and doesn't provide 2 IP addresses for whitelisting.

Three is correct. AWS Global Accelerator provides static IP addresses that act as a fixed entry point to application endpoints in a single or multiple AWS Regions. It uses two static anycast IP addresses.

Fourare incorrect. Route 53 geolocation-based routing does not provide automatic failover or 2 IP addresses.

Question 16 Answer(s):2

One is incorrect. AWS Lambda does not use as the public endpoint for API Gateway.

Twois correct. Amazon CloudFront does use as the public endpoint for API Gateway.

Three is incorrect. Amazon S3 does not use the public endpoint for API Gateway.

Fourare incorrect. Amazon ECS does not use as the public endpoint for API Gateway.

Question 17 Answer(s):3

One is incorrect. To provide low-latency access with Amazon S3, you would need to copy the videos to buckets in different regions worldwide and then create a mechanism for directing employees to the local copy.

Twoare incorrect. AWS Global Accelerator uses for directing users of applications to local points of presence around the world. It does not operate for accessing the content in S3. It does use with ELB and EC2.

Three is correct. CloudFront is a content delivery network and is ideal for this use case. It caches the content around the world, provides a single endpoint address, and uses a single source for the videos.

Fourare incorrect. AWS Lambda is a compute service and not suited to this use case.

Storage Answers

Question 1 Answer:

B. Amazon DynamoDB

Question 2 Answers:

A. Memcached

D. Redis

Question 3Answers:

A. Creating an Amazon S3 bucket

D. Configuring a VPC security group

E. Creating an Oracle RDS database

Question 4 Answer: C

The AWS Documentation mentions the below Linux Amazon Machine Images use one of two types of virtualization: paravirtual (PV) or hardware virtual machine (HVM). The main difference between PV and HVM AMIs is how they boot and whether they can take advantage of unique hardware extensions (CPU, network, and storage) for better performance.

Question 5 Answer:

B. Launch configuration

Question 6 Answer:

D. Enforces a minimum number of running Amazon EC2 instances.

E. Responds to changing conditions by adding or terminating Amazon EC2 instances.

F. Launches instances from a specified Amazon Machine Image (AMI).

Question 7 Answers:

C. Store the file in S3 Standard

Question 8 Answers:

A.   For files older than 30 days, create lifecycle rules to move these files to Amazon S3 Standard Infrequent Access and use Amazon Glacier to move files older than 40 days.

[Question 9 Answers:

D.   EBS Throughput Optimized HDD (st1)

Networking Answers

Question 1 Answer:A,D

A 500% increase is beyond the scope of a well-designed single server system to absorb unless it is already hugely overspecialized to accommodate this sort of burst load. An AWS solution for this situation might include S3 static web pages with client-side scripting to meet the high demand for information pages. Also, using a NoSQL database to collect customer registration for asynchronous processing and SQS backed by scalable compute to keep up with the requests. LightSail does provide a scalable provisioned service solution. However, these still need to be designed and planned by you and offer no significant advantage in this situation. A standby server is a good idea but will not help with the anticipated 500x load increase.

Question 2 Answer: A

Cognito will handle the user authentication; Lambda provides the serverless architecture that allows you to run your code without deploying it in an EC2 instance. Finally, S3 provides scalable object storage.

Question 3 Answer: D

The lease of an instance can only be changed between the "dedicated" lease hosting variants. It cannot change from the default rental hosting to the default rental hosting.

Question 4 Answer(s): A,C,D

Route 53 has the following routing strategies-simple, weighted, delayed, failover, multi-value response, and geographic location. And location

Question 5 Answer: B

Please note that if the data is in the same area, there will be no charge for transferring the data from EC2 to S3. AWS solution architects must know.

Question 6 Answer: B,D

CSV, YAML, XML, and JSON are all data formats (rather than languages). Still, only JSON and YAML can be used to create CloudFormation templates.

Question 7 Answer: C

The NACL's can be modified to be most secure by only denying the traffic from IP addresses.

Question 8 Answer: B

At present, the S3 category is; standard, standard infrequent access, an area infrequently accessed, reduced redundant storage, and Glacier & Glacier Deep Archive for archiving. Thin redundant storage is the only S3 category that does not provide 99.999999999% durability. Therefore, any answer that includes narrow redundant storage is incorrect.

Question 9 Answer: C, D

You should consider raising the bids of task nodes so that your nodes will not terminate, and even consider converting task nodes into on-demand instances to ensure that they are not released prematurely.

Question 10 Answer: A, B, C

The correct answers are Enterprise, Business, Developer, and the Basic free level. Remember that Free Tier is a Billing rebate, not an account or support level.

Question 11 Answer: A,D

All data transferred between any type of gateway appliance and AWS storage is encrypted using SSL. By default, all data stored by AWS

Storage Gateway in S3 is encrypted server-side with Amazon S3-Managed Encryption Keys (SSE-S3). Also, when using the file gateway, you can optionally configure each file share to have your objects encrypted with AWS KMS-Managed Keys using SSE-KMS.

Question 12 Answer: B,E

Network throughput is the apparent bottleneck. In this question, it will not tell you whether the proxy server is in a public subnet or a private subnet.

If it is in a public subnet, the size of the proxy server instance may not be large enough to handle its throughput. If the proxy server is in a private subnet, it must use a NAT instance or NAT gateway to communicate with the Internet. If it is a NAT instance, it may also be under-configured in terms of size. Therefore, you should increase the size of the proxy server and NAT solution.

Question 13 Answer: B, C,D

EBS, S3, and EFS all allow the user to configure encryption at rest using either the AWS Key Management Service (KMS) or, in some cases, using customer-provided keys. The exception on the list is ElastiCache for Memcached, which does not offer a native encryption service, although ElastiCache for Redis does.

Question 14 Answers: C,D

Trying to use S3 without File Gateway in front would be a significant impact on the user environment. Using File Gateway is the recommended way to use S3 with shared document pools. Life-cycle management and Infrequent Access storage are available for both S3 and EFS. A restriction, however, is that 'Using Amazon EFS with Microsoft Windows is not supported.' File Gateway does not support iSCSI on the client-side.

Question 15 Answers: C

Increasing the size increases both network throughput and compute power.

Content Delivery Answers

Question 1 Answer: A, B, D

Signed URLs and signed cookies are two ways to ensure that users can be authorized when they try to access files in an S3 bucket. One approach generates URLs, while the other creates unique cookies. Still, both require an application and policy to make to develop and manage these items.

Question 2 Answer: E

The Cloud Adoption Framework concentrates on the early stages of cloud adoption. Any reinvention of the business process is therefore not inherently considered as part of CAF.

Question 3 Answer: B

Amazon CloudFront has two types of distribution Web and RTMP. The limit of web distribution per account is 200, and RTMP per account is 100.

Question 4 Answer: B

Geo-restriction means you can restrict your content access in countries where you do not want to show your content. You can blacklist all countries you want to limit your scope, or you can whitelist the states for which you want to allow access to your content.

Question 5 Answer: A

Amazon CloudFront can work as an origin server or non-origin server. As an origin server, it includes Amazon EC2, Amazon S3 bucket, and Elastic Loud balancing or Route 53. As a non-origin server, it contains on-premises web servers.

Question 6 Answer: C

Through an invalidation API, you can remove malicious or harmful objects before their expiration time from all edge locations. That is an invalidation request.

Question 7 Answer: A

With CloudFront, you can use HTTP or HTTPS. Still, if you want to use SSL, then you need to use a default CloudFront URL that creates during the creation of distribution, or you can create a customized

URL with your SSL certificate. There are two separate ways to do Custom SSL depending on budget and outdated browser.

- Dedicated IP Custom SSL

- SNI (Server Name Identification) Custom SSL

Question 8 Answer: A

CloudFront supports GET, POST, HEAD, PUT, PATCH, DELETE, and OPTIONS HTTP requests. PUT, POST, PATCH, and DELETE bids, responses are not cached in CloudFront.

Question 9 Answer: D

Amazon Route 53, a DNS Web service, is scalable, highly available, and a cost-effective medium to direct the visitors to a website, a virtual server, or a load balancer.

Question 10 Answers:

You can use the Subnet Association tab to associate or disassociate subnets to the selected AWS Route Table.

Databases Answers

Question 1 Answer: B

Add multi-factor authentication (MFA) with a Cognito user pool is the correct answer.

Add multi-factor authentication (MFA) with a Cognito user pool is the solution that needs to implements to add the extra layer of security.

Question 2 Answer: D

AWS Certificate Manager is the correct answer. AWS Certificate Manager (ACM) makes it easy to provision, manage, and deploy SSL/TLS certificates on AWS managed resources.

Question 3 Answer: B

Traffic mirroring is the correct answer.

Traffic mirroring copies network traffic from an elastic network interface of an Amazon EC2 instance, and then you can then send the traffic to out-of-band security and monitoring appliances.

Question 4 Answer: D,E

Redis and Memcached are the two cache engines available in Elasticache.

Question 5 Answer:A

Rule: 100, Type: HTTP, Protocol: TCP, Port range: 80, Source: 0.0.0.0/0, Allow/Deny: ALLOW is the correct answer.

1) Rule: 100, Type: HTTP, Protocol: TCP, Port range: 443, Source: 0.0.0.0/0, Allow/Deny: ALLOW is incorrect because it uses the port 443, which is the HTTPS port

2) Rule: 100, Type: HTTP, Protocol: TCP, Port range: 53, Source: 0.0.0.0/0, Allow/Deny: ALLOW is incorrect because it uses the port 53, which is the DNS port

3) Rule: 100, Type: HTTP, Protocol: TCP, Port range: 22, Source: 0.0.0.0/0, Allow/Deny: ALLOW is incorrect because it uses the port 22, which is the SSH port

Question 6 Answer: D

Since there are some 'write' requests possible, 'read' replicas will not work. Amazon Redshift is an OLAP database that will allow writes too.

Question 7 Answer: A, B,C

Question 8 Answer: A

Use AWS Lambda environment variables is the correct answer.

Question 9 Answer: D

Amazon79EFS is a fully-managed service that makes it easy to set up, scale, and cost-optimize file storage in the Amazon Cloud.

Question 10 Answer: A

In the Security Group, add an Inbound SSH

rule is the correct answer. To resolve the issue, you need to add an Inbound SSH rule.

Question 11 Answer:B

Envelope encryption is the correct answer.

Question 12 Answer: A

Redis is a cache engine that uses for complex data types.

Question 13 Answer: A

Replication is one of the best approaches in case of failure of the node; through this, you can quickly recover the data. It supports high availability, separates the 'read' and 'write' workloads. In Memcached, there is no redundancy of data, while in Redis, there is replication.

Question 14 Answer:C

When you need to distribute your data over multiple nodes, it is also useful in cases where you need to run large nodes with multiple cores and threads.

Question 15 Answer: 3

One is incorrect. You cannot enable encryption for an existing database.

Twoare incorrect. You cannot restore the encrypted snapshot to the existing database instance.

Three is correct. You need to take an encrypted snapshot and create a new database instance from the photo.

Analytics Answers

Question 1 answer: C

Amazon Data Pipeline: for running ETL jobs

Amazon S3: for storing large volumes of data

Amazon EMR: for running Hadoop

Amazon Redshift: for data warehouse

Question 2 answer(s): A, B,E

In production environments, other clones of ElastiCache and CloudFront can all help improve site performance. Changing the auto-scaling strategy will not help improve performance time because the performance problem is likely to be the back end of the database rather than the front end. Pre-configured IOPS is not helpful because the bottleneck is memory rather than storage.

Question 3 answer: A

You have the chance to enable static web site hosting for S3 buckets. It can do via the properties option for the bucket. The endpoint of the bucket for static hosting will also configure.

Question 4 answer(s):B

AWS RDS database not fully managesthedatabase; it partially manages. For RDS, we still need to specify the server capacity, security group, etc. It is the point most of them are confused because they assume that RDS is the fully managed database. Even though the question doesn't ask about the type of database (NoSQL), the correct option is DynamoDB. For the fully managed option, it is Aurora and DynamoDB. So, the right choice in this question is DynamoDB. The link provides the full details of the product.

Question 5 answer(s):D

AWS Documentation Reference:

AWS re:INVENT 2017: Analyzing Streaming Data in Real-Time with Amazon Kinesis

Ingest and deliver raw data

*   CloudTrail provides continuous account activity logging

*   Events sent in real-time to Kinesis Data Firehose or Streams

*   Each event includes a timestamp, IAM user, AWS service name, API call, response, and more

Compute Operational Metrics in real-time

Amazon Kinesis data analytics compute metrics using SQL in real-time

Persist data for real-time dashboards

*   Use Kinesis Data Firehose to archive processed to in S3

*   Use AWS Lambda to deliver data to DynamoDB (or another database)

*   Open source or other tools to visualize the data

Question 6answer:A, C, D, F

B and E are features of the EMR File System (EMRFS).

AWS Documentation Reference: Work with Storage and File Systems

Question 7answer:A,B

AWS Documentation Reference:

Whitepaper: Streaming Data Solutions on AWS with Amazon Kinesis

You use Kinesis Streams if you want to do some custom processing with streaming data.

Question 8 answer:A,D

You would either user EBS or EFS. S3 is for object storage, not applications, and Glacier is for data archiving.

Question 9 answer: B

Question 10answer:A

AWS Documentation Reference: Whitepaper: Big_Data_Analytics_Options_on_AWS

Highly formatted canned Reports are not a scenario where Amazon Quicksight should uses.

Application Integration Answers

Question 1 Answer: 3, 5

Explanation:

The solutions architect must enable high availability for the architecture and ensure it is cost-effective. To help high availability, an

Amazon EC2 Auto Scaling group should create to add and remove instances across multiple availability zones.

Question 2 Answer: 3

Explanation:

The Amazon EC2-based application must be highly available and elastically scalable. Auto Scaling can provide the elasticity by dynamically launching and terminating instances based on demand. It can take place across availability zones for high availability.

Incoming connections can distribute to the instances by using an Application Load Balancer (ALB).

Question 3 Answer: 3

Explanation:

AWS Batch Multi-node parallel jobs enable you to run single jobs that span multiple Amazon EC2 instances. With the help of AWS Batch multi-node similar jobs, you can run large-scale, tightly coupled high-performance computing applications and distributed GPU model training without directly starting, configuring, and managing Amazon EC2 resources.

AWS Batch multi-node parallel jobs are compatible with any framework supporting IP-based communication between nodes, such as Apache MXNet, TensorFlow, Caffe2, or Message Passing Interface (MPI).

Question 4 Answer: 3

Explanation:

Amazon CloudTrail can be used to log activity on the reports. The critical difference between the two answers that include CloudTrail is that one references data events, whereas the other references management events.

Question 5 Answer: 4

Explanation:

The application is writing the files using API calls, which means it will be compatible with Amazon S3, which uses a REST API. S3 is a massively scalable key-based object store that is well-suited to allowing concurrent access to the files from many instances.

Amazon S3 will also be the most cost-effective choice. A rough calculation using the AWS pricing calculator shows the cost differences between 1TB of storage on EBS, EFS, and S3 Standard.

Question 6 Answer: 3

Explanation:

This question is merely asking you to work out the best compute service for the stated requirements. The essential requirements are that the compute service should be suitable for a workload that can range quite broadly in demand from no requests too large bursts of traffic.

AWS Lambda is an ideal solution as you pay when requests make, and it can quickly scale to accommodate the large bursts in traffic. Lambda works well with both API Gateway and Amazon RDS.

Question 7 Answer: 3

Explanation:

You can use the CloudWatch agent to collect both system metrics and log files from Amazon EC2 instances and on-premises servers. The agent supports both Windows Server and Linux and enables you to select the metrics to be collected, including sub-resource metrics such as per-CPU core.

There is now a unified agent, and previously there were monitoring scripts. Both of these tools can capture SwapUtilization metrics and send them to CloudWatch. It is the best way to get memory utilization metrics from Amazon EC2 instances.

Question 8 Answer: 3

Explanation:

Amazon ElastiCache is an in-memory database. With ElastiCache Memcached, there is no data replication or high availability. The Redis engine must uses, which does support both data replication and clustering.

Question 9 Answer: 2,4

AWS Global Accelerator uses static IP addresses as fixed entry points for your application. You can migrate up to two /24 IPv4 address ranges and choose which /32 IP addresses to use when creating your accelerator.

This solution ensures the company can continue using the same IP addresses. They can direct traffic to the application endpoint in the AWS Region closest to the end-user.

Question 10 Answer: 1

Explanation:

The best option is to configure the database security group to allow traffic from the application security group. You can also define the destination port as the database port. This setup will allow any instance that is launched and attached to this security group to connect to the database.

Question 11Answer: 3

Explanation:

Amazon FSx for Windows File Server provides fully managed, highly reliable file storage accessible over the industry-standard Server Message Block (SMB) protocol. It is built on Windows Server, delivering a wide range of administrative features such as user quotas, end-user file restore, and Microsoft Active Directory (AD) integration. It offers single-AZ and multi-AZ deployment options, fully managed backups, and encryption of data at rest and transit.

Question12:Answer: 2

Explanation:

CloudWatch Events rules can use to set automatic email notifications of medium to high severity results to an email address of your choice.You simply create an Amazon SNS topic and then associate it with an Amazon CloudWatch events rule.

Question 13 Answer: 2,4

Explanation:

None of the options present theright solution for specifying permissions required to write and modify objects. That requirement needs to be taken care of separately. The other conditions are to prevent accidental deletion and ensure that all versions of the document are available.

Question 14 Answer:2

Explanation:

The most cost-effective solution is to first store the data in S3 Standard-IA, where it will frequently access for the first three months. After three months expires, transition the data to S3 Glacier,storing at a lower cost for the remainder of the seven years. Expedited retrieval can bring retrieval times down to 1-5 minutes.

Question 15 Answer: 2

Explanation:

An Amazon Simple Queue Service (SQS) can be used to offload and decouple the long-running requests. They can then be processed asynchronously by separate EC2 instances. It is the best way to reduce the overall latency introduced by the long-running API call.

Question 16 Answer: 3

Explanation:

The Redis authentication token allows Redis to ask for permission (password) before allowing the client to execute commands, thereby improving data security. You can require users to enter a token on a Redis server protected by a receipt. For this reason, when creating a replication group or cluster, please include the parameter --auth-token (API: AuthToken) in the correct ticket. Besides, it should use in the replication group or all subsequent commands of the replication group.

CORRECT: "Redis AUTH command" is the right answer.

INCORRECT: "AWS Directory Service" is incorrect. It is a managed Microsoft Active Directory service and cannot add password protection to Redis.

INCORRECT: "AWS IAM Policy" is incorrect. You cannot use an IAM policy to enforce a password on Redis.

INCORRECT: "VPC Security Group" is wrong. A security group protects the network layer; it does not affect application authentication.

AWS Security, Identity & Compliance Answers

Question 1 answer:

Amazon Cognito manages authentication and authorization for your public-facing programs.

Question 2 answer:

The team members should place in groups as users with specific roles assigned to each of them, including the period of the day to access the platform.

Question 3 answer:

Amazon Web Services (AWS) should apply usage limits to most of its infrastructure and resources. But, users can request for such limitations to lift before accessing such services.

Question 4 answer:

Infrastructure as a service (IaaS) provides users access to the virtual components of a provider's physical resources. These customers handle their infrastructures the same way they would their physical servers.

Question 5 answer:

The method of authentication for accessing files is called access keys.

Question 6 answer:

The method of end-to-end encryption that protects data or files at every stage of its lifecycle is called client-side encryption.

Question 7 answer: 1

Explanation:

One is correct. The maximum filesize for Amazon S3 objects is five terabytes.

Twoare incorrect. It is the minimum file size possible in Amazon S3.

Three is incorrect. 5GB is not the maximum file size possible in Amazon S3.

Fourare incorrect. There is a limit on the maximum file size for objects in Amazon S3

Question 8 answer:

The main advantage of resource tags is to view and manage resources on active accounts, mainly if applied with consistent naming or descriptive patterns.

Question 9 Answer: 2

To specify permissions for a specific task on Amazon ECS, you should use IAM Roles for Tasks. The permissions policy can be applied to tasks when creating the task definition, or by using an IAM task role override using the AWS CLI or SDKs. The taskRoleArn parameter uses to specify the policy.

CORRECT: "Create an IAM policy with permissions to DynamoDB and assign It to a task using the taskRoleArn parameter" is the right answer.

Question 10 Answer: 1

Explanation:

You need to assign the role to the Lambda function, NOT to the DynamoDB table.

CORRECT: "Creating an Identity and Access Management (IAM) role with the required permissions to access DynamoDB tables and assigning the part to the Lambda function is the correct answer.

CPSIA information can be obtained
at www.ICGtesting.com
Printed in the USA
LVHW011150201120
672013LV00006B/832